The Multiple-Cat Family

SHEILA WEBSTER BONEHAM, Ph.D.

The Multiple-Cat Family

Project Team
Editor: Craig Sernotti
Copy Editor: Stephanie Fornino
Indexer: Lucie Haskins
Interior Design: Leah Lococo Ltd. and Stephanie Krautheim
Design Layout: Stephanie Krautheim

T.F.H. Publications
President/CEO: Glen S. Axelrod
Executive Vice President: Mark E. Johnson
Publisher: Christopher T. Reggio
Production Manager: Kathy Bontz

T.F.H. Publications, Inc.
One TFH Plaza
Third and Union Avenues
 Neptune City, NJ 07753

Discovery Communications, Inc. Book Development Team
Marjorie Kaplan, President, Animal Planet Media
Carol LeBlanc, Vice President, Licensing
Elizabeth Bakacs, Vice President, Creative Services
Sue Perez-Jackson, Director, Licensing
Bridget Stoyko, Designer
Caitlin Erb, Manager, Licensing

 Exterior design ©2008 Discovery Communications, Inc. Animal Planet, logo and Animusings are trademarks of Discovery Communications, Inc., used under license. All rights reserved. animalplanet.com

08 09 10 11 12 1 3 5 7 9 8 6 4 2

Printed and bound in China

Library of Congress Cataloging-in-Publication Data

Boneham, Sheila Webster, 1952-

 Multiple-cat family / Sheila Webster Boneham.
     p. cm. – (Animal Planet pet care library)

 Includes index.

 ISBN 978-0-7938-3798-4 (alk. paper)

 1. Cats. I. Title.

 SF447.B615 2008

 636.8–dc22

                    2008009914

tfh

The Leader in Responsible Animal Care for Over 50 Years!®

www.tfh.com

Table of **Contents**

Chapter 1

A Clowder of

Cats

Tabbies and torties and smokes—oh my! Cats come in a rainbow of colors, long hair and short, green eyes and blue. They have distinct personalities, preferences, and quirks. With all those variations in a companionable package, it's no wonder that about half of the 35.4 million cat-owning households in the United States have more than one.

Perhaps you already live with a clowder (a group) of cats. Or maybe you're thinking of adding a second cat to your family or of going from zero to two in one adoption. Whatever your multi-cat status, there's something in this book for you. My goal is to suggest ways to make living with multiple felines smoother and easier for you and your cats so that you can focus on the good stuff.

Do You Really Want More Than One?

We could fill a whole book with reasons for having more than one cat. If you are gone from home for long hours, your cat may be lonely and may enjoy the company of his own kind. If your cat is getting on in years, he may be rejuvenated by a kitten in the family, and you may feel less apprehensive about his advancing age.

On the other hand, some cats are very solitary or territorial and really prefer to be the only cat in the home. While most cats will eventually adjust to the presence of another cat, establishing a peaceful coexistence may take some time and effort if one or more of the parties is an isolationist. (See Chapter 4.)

Costs

Even if everyone gets along, there are some things to consider before taking on an additional cat. Although cats are not the most expensive of pets, responsible care does cost money. The more cats you have, the more money you will spend to take proper care of them. They need nutritious food (see Chapter 5), and they need regular veterinary care. (See Chapter 7.) The more cats you have, the more litter boxes and litter you will need. (See Chapter 6.) And of course, there are all the other goodies that cat people buy

What's Good About Having More Than One Cat

Here are some reasons why the cost and cleanup of more than one cat are worthwhile, aside from the extra love!

- Cats who have the company of another cat (or, sometimes, a dog) are less likely to misbehave out of boredom.
- Cats who have feline company are less likely to suffer from separation anxiety or depression.
- Cats who are raised with other cats are more adaptable to changes in their environments and to newcomers and visitors.

There are benefits to keeping multiple cats together, but some may prefer to be by themselves. Monitor their interactions and react accordingly.

their cats—toys, treats, cat trees and condos, beds, and so forth.

Cleaning Up After Your Cat

More cats also require more of your time, and I don't mean just for play and cuddles. You'll need to clean those extra litter boxes and food bowls. You'll have to vacuum more often to manage the extra hair your cats shed. Each cat needs to be groomed regularly to keep him healthy. (See Chapter 7.) And of course, you will want to spend some time each day with each cat to reinforce the bond between you.

Cat Licensing

In some communities, your decision about adding another cat to your household may be made for you by the law. Licensing laws do apply to cats in most places, and many communities have laws limiting the number of

pets people are allowed to own. (See Chapter 2.)

If you decide that you really want more than one cat and know that you can provide for each cat's needs, you aren't alone—49 percent of cat owners have two or more cats. Now it's time to think about what you want in your next cat.

Choosing the Cat To Bring Home

If you already have at least one cat, you probably have some idea of the traits you want—and the ones you don't want—in your next feline companion. To paraphrase many a mother's advice on choosing a spouse, it's just as easy to fall in love with a cat whose traits suit you as with one who is a long way from being your ideal cat. Let's look at the pros and cons of various feline traits.

Housekeeping Tips

We've all heard about homes where the smell of litter boxes assaults visitors at the door, and blankets of cat hair cover floors, furniture, and guests. Living with more than one cat does not have to be a smelly, hairy mess, though. Here are some tips for keeping a cleaner house even with multiple cats.

- Keep litter boxes clean, and get control of inappropriate elimination immediately.

- Don't leave cat food sitting around—it attracts vermin.

- Brush all your cats several times a week—daily in the spring and fall when they are shedding.

- Vacuum as frequently as necessary to keep hair and dander from covering your home.

FAMILY-FRIENDLY TIP

Cats, Kids, and Community

Cats can be wonderful childhood friends, and having a pet can help children learn many important life lessons. But before you add an additional cat to your household, be sure that he will be welcomed by the adults in the family, too. It isn't fair to the cat or child to place all responsibility for an animal on a child's shoulders. Adults must model responsible pet care.

Coats

Long, luxurious coats are gorgeous, but they come with a price. Although a few semi-long and long-haired breeds require little grooming, most long-haired cats need to be brushed every day to keep their coats from tangling or matting and to reduce shedding. Long-haired cats are also more prone to hairballs (see Chapter 7) than are most shorthairs. If you already have a long-haired cat, you might want a shorthair to reduce your grooming load and for the variation in looks the different coats provide.

Male or Female

Although people often have strong opinions about whether males or females make the best pets, the individual cat is much more important than the sex. As long as all your cats are spayed or neutered, they can get along with members of the same or opposite sex.

Kittens

Kittens are cute, but they need extra care, supervision, protection, and some training. Many kittens go through a high-energy adolescence, getting into everything and pestering everyone. When you adopt an adult, his size, color, coat length, and personality are all fully formed. And don't worry that he won't bond to you—adult cats seem to understand and appreciate a new home where they're loved. A kitten might adjust to your current cats a little more quickly (although the adults might not be so pleased!), but with careful introductions (see Chapter 4), adults usually accept one another, too.

Personalities

Personality is probably the most important trait in a pet. Do you want a "Velcro" cat who seeks human and feline companionship, or do you want a more independent character?

If you have children, a highly social, easygoing, playful cat is what you need. The cats themselves pick their friends by personality and behavioral traits, not looks. Very different personalities may clash—a bouncy, pushy cat may provoke a more reserved housemate to an aggressive reaction or drive him into seclusion. Cats with similar approaches to life generally get along better.

You and Your Cats

Whatever your taste is in felines, there are cats to fit the bill—fluffy and plush, sleek and lithe, rambunctious or calm, gregarious or standoffish. Maybe you know exactly what you want. Maybe you can't make up your mind and opt for one of each. It's also quite possible that your cats have chosen you. Whatever your reasons for increasing your feline family, my hope is that the remainder of this book will help you all live happily ever after.

Cats have varying hair lengths. Picking the ones you decide to bring into your home carefully as opposed to impulsively will help reduce the time you must devote to grooming.

Chapter 2

Cats in the

Human
Community

Cats outdoors seem to inhabit the shadows,
moving quietly and trying not to draw attention
to themselves. Their low-key presence makes it
easy to forget that cats do have an impact on the
neighborhood, whether you live on a farm, in the
suburbs, or in an urban high-rise. But the fact
is that your cats do affect your neighbors, both
human and animal. The more cats you have, the
more profound their effect.

Impact of Cats on Wildlife

Free-roaming domestic cats have a profound impact on wildlife. Obviously, if you allow more than one cat to hunt around your home, the impact they make will be even greater. Studies show that 60 to 70 percent of animals killed by domestic cats are small mammals, and 20 to 30 percent are birds. Cats also kill amphibians, reptiles, and insects. Not only do they affect the prey species that they hunt and kill, they essentially steal food from native predators. Because your cats hunt for fun and you shield them from hunger, disease, parasites, infection, and the limitations that come with injury, your cats have a serious advantage over wild hunters. Even if your cats are vaccinated and healthy, they can spread diseases against which wild animals have no protection. On the other hand, your cats can easily contract diseases and parasites, which they will carry home and share with your other cats, and in some cases, your other pets and you. So think carefully about the cost of "freedom" before you let your cats out the door.

Indoors or Out?

Should cats be kept indoors, or should they be allowed to roam outside? That's one of the most emotionally charged questions faced by cat owners and their neighbors alike. There's no doubt that your cats are safer in the house, where their exposure to motor vehicles, animal attacks, infectious diseases, harmful chemicals, parasites, and abusive people is reduced or eliminated. There's also no doubt that cats have an effect on their environments and can be a major source of conflict among neighbors. Still, like many people, you may feel that your cats need some time outdoors to hunt chipmunks and bugs in the fresh air and nap in the sun.

There are ways to compromise, letting your cats have some outdoor time without allowing them to wander free, but these compromises require your time and/or money. Some people leash train their cats and take them for walks. That can work if you're willing to walk one or two at a time, but if you have several cats, "walkies" could take over your life. Besides, some cats aren't so keen on the idea. If you have the space and money, you could build a special fenced-in area that will keep your cats confined outdoors. The top, side, and bottom edges must be secure to prevent escape. Smooth-sided fencing material, such as vinyl, is hard to climb, and a lip angled in around the top edge will stop most climbers. Some people go the extra step and stretch wire mesh or similar material across the top of the cats' outdoor area.

Legal Issues

Most places have laws affecting pet owners and ownership, and every year more laws are passed. Although people often think that such laws pertain to dogs only, many also apply to cats. Some laws are beneficial to responsible pet owners and their neighbors alike. Others are excessively restrictive without providing any real benefit to most members of the community. If you want to protect your rights as a cat owner, know your local laws and keep track of proposed laws. Your local animal control or city or county government office should be able to provide you with a copy of the legal code applying to animals where you live. Find out where political candidates stand on pet laws and vote. That's the best way to protect your cats and your rights.

Now let's look at a few of the more common types of laws affecting cats and their people.

Licensing

Many jurisdictions require pet owners to purchase licenses for their cats and dogs. Revenue from pet licenses often helps support local animal shelters, although it usually covers only a small portion of the annual funding. Because proof of vaccination is nearly always required to purchase a license, licensing in theory promotes rabies vaccinations and thereby cuts down on the spread of the disease, reducing the risk of exposure for people. The catch is that often the people who comply with the licensing laws are already responsible cat owners who regularly vaccinate their pets. Some people see licensing as government intrusion and

an unnecessary expense and so don't license their cats, especially if they have more pets than the law allows.

You do, however, gain some benefits from licensing your cats. A license tag attached to a cat's collar usually improves your chances of getting him back if he becomes lost. It may even save his life—in some places where the number of strays overwhelms the available kennel space, cats and dogs with no license tags are euthanized very quickly. And of course, having your cats properly licensed puts you in compliance with the law.

License costs vary from municipality to municipality, so you will have to check with your local authorities. Often it is much less expensive to license altered (spayed and neutered) pets, and many jurisdictions offer discounts or

Your cats should wear collars and ID tags if you allow them to go outdoors.

13

Cats in the Human Community

even free licensing to certain members of the public. It can't hurt to ask.

Confinement Laws

In many places, it is against local and state law to allow pets, including cats, to run loose. Even some subdivisions include provisions against free-roaming animals in their covenants (which may or may not be legally binding). If you allow your cats to roam, you could be subject to various fines. Worse, you could lose your cats and provide ammunition for those who would further limit our right to own pets. So please think carefully before you make your cats fugitives from the law.

To be sure, there are good reasons not to let your cats run loose. Cats at large are vulnerable to many dangers. (See "Outdoor Hazards" later in this chapter.) They also help spread diseases and parasites they've picked up in their travels, and they often have profound negative effects on wild animals.

Keep in mind that, despite their distant relationship to lions and tigers and their own endearing "wild" streaks, your cats are not wild animals who need to be free. They are as domesticated as we are, and they need the safety of the home.

Numbers Limits

Many communities now limit the number of pets a person can legally own. Supporters of these laws claim that the limits prevent pets from becoming nuisances. Realistically, limit laws do not address the real problem—irresponsible owners. One cat running loose, killing songbirds at the neighbors' feeders and using the neighbors' petunias as his personal litter box, is more of a nuisance than several cats living inside the right home. If you are a responsible owner, you know your limits and you control your pets.

Limits on pet ownership are very difficult to enforce, and they encourage otherwise law-abiding pet owners to break the law. Although laws limiting pet ownership solely on the basis of numbers have been challenged

You may not mind your cats being outside, but your neighbors may, especially if they lounge on your neighbor's outdoor furniture or adopt a flowerbed as their litter box.

successfully in several communities around the country, there have also been many sad cases of people having to give up a cat or two because they had, say, six cats instead of the legal five. You may think that numbers limits don't affect you—you only have two or three cats. Please think again. The numbers used to establish limits are arbitrary, and if the limit can be set at five today, tomorrow it may be lowered to two. Or one. Again, protect your rights to responsible cat ownership by knowing what laws are being proposed in your community and who supports them. Vote.

Your Cats and Your Neighbors

Cats can cause considerable friction among neighbors—another good reason not to let your pets run loose. Even die-hard animal lovers will react with anger if someone else's cats hunt or go potty in their yards. And although it's hard to believe, there are people who don't find our cats as charming as we do under any circumstances. A look from the other side of the lot line may make the neighbors' view easier to understand.

Fences may make good neighbors, but so does responsible pet ownership. Don't let your cats take the blame for behavior that is your responsibility.

Keeping Your Cats Safe

We think of our homes as safe havens. But please don't take the safety of your house and yard for granted. Unless you have already done some serious kitty-proofing, you probably live with many

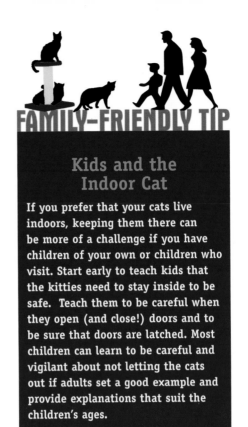

FAMILY-FRIENDLY TIP

Kids and the Indoor Cat

If you prefer that your cats live indoors, keeping them there can be more of a challenge if you have children of your own or children who visit. Start early to teach kids that the kitties need to stay inside to be safe. Teach them to be careful when they open (and close!) doors and to be sure that doors are latched. Most children can learn to be careful and vigilant about not letting the cats out if adults set a good example and provide explanations that suit the children's ages.

potential dangers for your cats. Some are obvious—products that are labeled as poisons, for instance. Others are less clear, even when present. For instance, many common house and garden plants are lethal to cats when ingested. The scented oils used in potpourri and other fragrance products are toxic. Nicotine in tobacco products and in nicotine patches or gum can kill a cat. Kittens, especially, are notorious for falling into nasty things like motor oil. Clearly, danger can be found where we least expect it, and curiosity really can kill your cats.

Dangers in the Home

The chances that your cats will find trouble increase along with the number of cats. So while it's important to kitty-proof your home for a single feline companion, it's even more critical when you have two or more, especially if any of them are curious kittens or adolescents with lots of energy and little experience. Here are some things you can do to make your cats' living quarters safer:

• Shield electrical, telephone, and cable wires from teeth and claws. You can purchase specially made sheaths in many computer, hardware, and home stores, or make your own with PVC pipe cut to length.

• Be sure that all surfaces that might attract adventurous felines are secure. You don't want a multi-cat chase up the bookcase and over the end table to result in a crash.

• Keep foods and their containers safely locked away. Chocolate, coffee, tea, and other products containing caffeine are dangerous for cats and can cause problems ranging from diarrhea and vomiting to seizures and death. Raisins and grapes can cause fatal kidney damage. Swallowing foil, plastic wrappers, strings, and other packaging materials can injure delicate tissues and cause blockages in the esophagus, stomach, and intestines. Raw or leftover meats may contain dangerous bacteria or parasites.

• Keep toilet lids closed. A curious kitten can fall into the bowl and drown. An older cat could probably climb out but will likely pick up bacteria and/or toxic residue left by toilet bowl cleaners.

• Pick up small objects that a cat might play with or swallow. Rubber bands, coins, pins, needles, thread, yarn, string, dental floss, fish hooks, fishing line, and so on are all potentially deadly for your cats.

• Remove loops from blind or drapery cords. Playful cats can get tangled in loops and be injured or strangled.

• Make sure that all door and window latches and screens are secure so that no one can get out or fall.

• Safeguard open flames and hot surfaces. Cats like to be warm, but a hot stove or a burning candle can cause serious injuries.

• Keep your washer and dryer closed,

and check inside before you close them and turn them on.

- Keep hidey-holes like cupboards, closets, refrigerators, and freezers closed (and make sure that they are free of cats before you close them). Seal or remove the doors from any you don't use to keep clever claws from pulling them open.

- Ensure that there are no cats near the mechanisms of sofa beds, reclining chairs, and similar furniture before you operate them.

- Be particularly careful around holidays, which pose special hazards to your cats. Avoid decorating with tinsel, ribbons, and other things your cats might swallow. Shield electrical cords. Be cautious about using breakable decorations. Keep food hazards where your cats can't get to them. Be especially cautious when people are coming and going—the last thing you want on a holiday is a lost cat.

Outdoor Hazards

The outdoors may be great in some ways, but the modern world holds many dangers for free-roaming cats. Motor vehicles kill and maim thousands of cats every year. Animals, both wild and domestic, also pose a danger for cats on the loose. Some dogs will attack and kill cats, and in many parts of North America—including urban and suburban areas—coyotes are serious predators of domestic felines. Cats sometimes fight with other cats, sustaining serious injuries

Kittens, Seniors, and the Great Outdoors

Like all young animals, kittens lack experience and good sense and in the twitch of a tail can find themselves in serious trouble. They climb too high. They squeeze into places they shouldn't. They fall into hazardous substances (like cans of motor oil). They venture into unsafe places, where they can be hit by cars or attacked by other animals. Seniors have the sense and experience of a lifetime, but as age impairs their sensory organs and their reflexes, they gradually become more vulnerable. Even if you decide that your cats should go outdoors, be more cautious with the young and the old.

in the process. People sometimes betray the trust cats place in our species, intentionally injuring or killing unprotected cats.

Even animals that your cats see as prey can hurt them, either directly with bites and scratches or indirectly by transmitting infections, diseases, and parasites. Domestic cats contract rabies more often than any other domestic animals. But rabies isn't the only disease cats can acquire from other animals, and any contact with wild animals and unvaccinated domestic animals, especially other cats, puts your own cat family at risk. (For more information on infectious diseases and parasites, including rabies, see Chapter 7.)

Hazardous chemicals are another common problem for cats on the loose. They can easily be tempted by poisons designed to attract their intended victims—rodenticides, slug bait, coyote bait, and some insecticides taste good and are just as deadly for cats as for vermin. Many cats are attracted to certain toxic plants. Puddles of antifreeze taste good, and they kill. Cats also ingest poisons inadvertently when they lick themselves clean after exposure to petroleum products, lawn treatments, toxic plants, cleaning products, and other poisonous substances. You can keep such hazards locked away in your own home and yard, but you can't control what other people leave within easy reach.

Freedom has a certain philosophical ring, but the truth is that cats who roam free usually live shorter lives and all too often die violent deaths. If you provide them with company and an enriched environment, your cats can live happily inside your home, and they will be safer and healthier there.

Don't Leave Home Without It

One of the most important tools you have for keeping your cats safe is up-to-date identification. Even if you routinely keep your cats in, the day may come when one or more of them slip out. Tags on their collars may get them back home to you, so each cat should wear a collar with his current license and rabies tags and an identification tag with your name and phone number. Many people now also include an e-mail address. If your cat is registered with one of the national services for lost-and-found pets, include that tag as well. Unfortunately, collars and tags can be lost or removed, so a form of permanent identification is a good idea as well. Not only can it help you get a lost cat back, but it proves that this is in fact *your* cat.

The best form of permanent identification for a cat is a microchip (technically known as a transponder). Microchips are tiny electronic transponders about the size of a grain of rice that are injected under

the skin over the shoulder blades. Each microchip transmits a unique numerical code, which you must register with a database that links you to your cat. The microchip is read at close range by a handheld scanning device. Unlike the transponders used by biologists on wild animals, microchips do not transmit a signal that can be located at a distance. However, they do provide permanent identification and proof of ownership.

Your veterinarian can chip your cats, and many shelters and other organizations offer microchip clinics. If you have microchips inserted into more than one cat at a time, you may be able to get a discount. Some shelters, rescuers, and breeders microchip their cats before placing them in new homes, in which case you will need to transfer the registration to your name. Even if the breeder or rescuer wants to remain on the registration as a backup, you need to give the database your own information.

When you take each cat for his annual checkup, ask your vet to scan for the microchip to be sure that it's still working. If your contact information changes, don't forget to notify the database registry. It's a good idea to register all your pets with the same database, if possible. For more information, ask your vet or area shelter, or contact the companies directly.

How to Find a Missing Cat

As was already mentioned, no matter how careful you are, sooner or later

Where to Learn More About Microchips

The two major microchips registries in the US are:

- AVID®, www.avidid.com, 1-800-336-AVID

- HomeAgain®, www.akc.org, then click on Companion Animal Recovery, 1-800-2FIND-PET

one or more of your cats may slip out and get lost. And if you let your cats go outdoors, there may come a day when one of them doesn't come home. Even if they are picked up and placed in a shelter, many lost cats are euthanized without seeing their homes again. That's why it's important to be proactive if someone goes missing.

Before you do anything else, make sure that your cat is really gone. More than one feline felon has given his owner palpitations by watching from a hidey-hole while the frantic human searches high and low. You probably know where your cats like to hide, but just in case, here are some places to check:

- Drawers and the spaces behind them. Check furniture and filing cabinets. Check them all, even if you don't think the culprit would fit—cats can squeeze into surprisingly tiny spaces.

- Bookcases, including upper shelves, and behind books and decorations.

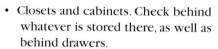

Lost cats can be found if you act quickly.

- Closets and cabinets. Check behind whatever is stored there, as well as behind drawers.

- Inside, behind, under, and on top of the washer, dryer, refrigerator, oven, dishwasher, and any other appliances you have.

- Places where you've done any remodeling or redecorating that offered access to the spaces behind walls, ceilings, floors, crawl spaces, or air ducts. I once pulled out a toilet-paper holder to paint a bathroom and watched in dismay as my Malcolm's striped tail disappeared through the hole. It took a trip to the store and a can of salmon to coax the little devil out!

- Inside any upholstered furniture, mattresses, or box springs that have holes in them or access from underneath.

- Fireplaces, wood boxes, wood stoves, chimneys, and similar "caves."

- Under, behind, and on top of furniture, including hidden supports.

- Inside boxes, suitcases, flowerpots, and similar containers. If it has a lid, open it—maybe your missing cat already did.

- Inside your car, including up under the hood, if your cat has access to the garage or outdoors. Our cat Mary used to snooze on the front seat of the car if she could squeeze through the window.

- Anywhere else that you can't easily see into—laundry baskets full of clothes, the clothes hamper, a dollhouse, cat carriers, or your dog's crate.

If you've looked everywhere you can think of and still haven't found your cat, there are several things you can do to increase the odds of a happy ending. Probably the single most important thing is to realize that *anyone* can have a cat go missing, and plan ahead by providing all your cats with identification.

The faster you act, the better the chances that you will find your missing cat or cats. If possible, visit all shelters and veterinarians in the area and give them as much information on each cat as possible—ideally, you can provide a photo and your cat's microchip and license tag numbers. If you can't visit, call. Describe each missing cat by sex, coat length, and color, and give microchip and license tag numbers. Don't assume that people, even in vets' offices and shelters, will know what a particular breed looks like or a technical name for a color or pattern. If you have a blue Persian, tell them he's a gray long-haired cat. Don't assume either that the person you speak to really knows whether a cat matching your description is in the facility. If possible, visit your area shelters at least once a day, or have someone who knows your cat help you with some of the visits. Vet offices, and especially shelters, are often chaotic, and if the staff is large, those who answer the phone may not know about all the animals in residence. You need to see for yourself whether they have your missing cat.

Make up posters with photos of your cat (in color, if possible), information on where and when he was lost, and your telephone number. Put them up around the area where your cat was last seen and at nearby stores and coffeehouses that offer bulletin boards. If legal in your area, place posters around your neighborhood. Take copies to area shelters and veterinarians—a picture posted where people see it will be much more effective than a phoned-in description. Ask the principals of local schools for permission to hang your posters—children often know more than adults do about animals that are hanging around the neighborhood. Call the local newspapers (all of them!) and

run a lost ad. Hope that your cat or cats will be home before the ad appears.

Be Responsible

Cats are integral members of human communities and have been for thousands of years. Responsible care for our cats, coupled with respect for our human neighbors, will help ensure that domestic cats remain where they belong—in our homes and at our sides.

Chapter 3

Your Social Cats

Although you and your cats share your home and your hearts, in many ways you live in parallel universes. It's easy to attribute human senses and motivations to our pets, but the fact is that your cats perceive the world differently than you do. Ways of seeing, hearing, smelling, tasting, feeling, and processing information are different in our two species. It's really quite miraculous that very different animals—felines, humans, maybe a canine or two, and possibly others—are able to share living space successfully, respect and love one another, and communicate reasonably well.

No matter how long we live with cats or how many cats we've known and loved, there's always more to learn. It may be tempting sometimes to think of them as what are popularly called "fur babies," those soft creatures curled on our laps and beds. But cats are far more interesting if we see them as cats, with their supremely feline senses and sensibilities. It's even more important to do so in a multi-cat home. Your cats may meet you halfway and sometimes seem to be half human, but they interact with each other purely as cats. Let's peek into their feline world.

Feline Chemistry

To understand much of your cats' behavior, you have to understand that they live in a world of scent that we can only imagine. The chemicals that make up various odors enable your cats to give and receive information about each other—who they are, how they feel, when they were here. They also use scent to learn about you, other family members, and their prey. Cats also take pleasure in many odors, although chances are we wouldn't agree with their taste in fragrances.

Cats, like all animals, produce and excrete chemicals called pheromones from special glands located on various parts of their bodies. Pheromones affect other animals of the same species, stimulating the brain to provoke a variety of behaviors ranging from fear, aggression, and avoidance to pleasure, sexual attraction, and a sense of well-being. When your cats rub their faces on you, one another, your furniture, doorframes, and so on, they deposit pheromones that seem to have a calming effect. When they scratch, they not only keep their claws in shape but also deposit scent from glands in

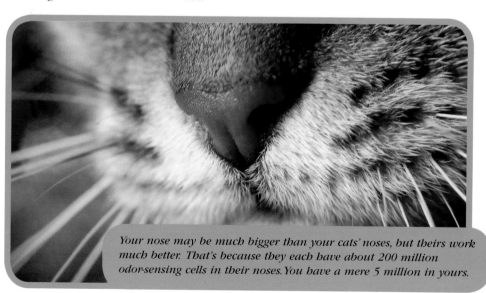

Your nose may be much bigger than your cats' noses, but theirs work much better. That's because they each have about 200 million odor-sensing cells in their noses. You have a mere 5 million in yours.

Listen Up

Have you ever wondered what your cats seem to be listening to when you can't hear a thing? Chances are they're tuning in to high-frequency sounds that are beyond the human range of perception. Cats hear about ten octaves—two more than we humans can perceive. The feline sensitivity to higher frequencies is a survival skill, enabling cats to hear sounds made by small rodents and by newborn kittens. They aren't as good as we are at distinguishing between tones, but the sensitivity of their inner ears and the mobility of their pinnae (outer ears) make them much better at locating the source of a sound and at differentiating among sounds from multiple sources.

their pads. When they urinate, defecate, or spray, they deposit pheromones that delineate their territories.

Your Territorial Cats

Cats, like many predators, are territorial animals. If your cats lived in the wild, each of them would live and hunt alone in a specific area—his territory. The size of this territory would depend in large part on the amount of food available. In times of plenty, the cats wouldn't need to wander so far to find food as in leaner times.

Feline territories often overlap, and the cats operate on sort of a time-share basis, each of them visiting different parts of the territory at specific times. Each cat marks the boundaries of his territory by rubbing and scratching and sometimes by urinating, defecating, and spraying. This behavior is like a bulletin board where other cats learn about the age, gender, and health status of the marking cat. More importantly, marking lets all the cats know what time each of the others uses each place, allowing them to avoid encounters that might lead to fights and injuries.

Although they don't have to hunt for their meals, your cats do establish territories in your home. Hopefully they don't mark by scratching and spraying your furniture (see Chapter 6) but by rubbing with their faces and bodies and scratching "legal" scratching stations. If you keep track, you will no doubt see that your cats rest in different places on a regular rotation.

Stress in Your Multi-Cat Home

I saw a T-shirt recently that said, "You can never have too many cats." Cute, but is it true? Each additional cat adds to your expenses, of course—food, litter, equipment, veterinary care, and other things all cost money. The more cats you have, the more time you must spend on cat-related work: shopping, feeding, washing food and water

Your cats will establish territories around your home. Some of your cats may share a territory, while others may be the lone cat in the room—it all depends on their personalities.

bowls, cleaning litter boxes, brushing, vacuuming, and so on. There may even be a legal limit on how many cats you can have. (See Chapter 2.) All of these considerations are important, but they are human issues. What about the feline perspective? Can a cat have too many housemates?

In a word, yes. How many cats are too many depends on various factors, including how much space you have, how you arrange the cat things like food and litter boxes, the general atmosphere of your home, the genders and reproductive status of your cats, and of course, their individual temperaments.

Most cats will adapt to living with other cats to some degree, but like any social group, tensions can arise for many reasons. Also, the more cats you have, the more likely they will have

some squabbles. As was mentioned earlier, cats are by nature territorial. If they feel crowded and unable to define territories, they experience stress. When they are under stress, they are more likely to exhibit a range of undesirable behaviors. In fact, behaviorists believe that stress is at the root of most behavior problems in cats. But what is stress? And specifically, what causes stress in cats?

What Is Stress?

The term "stress," as used by veterinarians and behaviorists, refers to psychological and physiological changes that occur when an animal becomes frightened. When one of your cats feels threatened, his body reacts in preparation for a response. His eyes open wide and his pupils dilate to let him see the threat more clearly. His

How to Make Life
More Comfortable for Multiple Cats

have, or are planning to have, more than one cat in your home, here are some
nat will help make your environment more feline friendly.

all your cats spayed or neutered.

each cat some individual attention every day.

oduce newcomers slowly and carefully. (See Chapter 4.)

ide as many litter boxes as you have cats, plus one extra, and place them in di:
s of the house. Clean all litter boxes at least once a day. (For more on litter box
ter 6.)

ide hidey-holes where your cats can be alone. Chances are each cat will stake c
—you can help by providing some soft bedding to make it comfy.

ide dog-free and child-free zones so that your cats can be alone when they wa:
h your children to leave the cats alone when they are sleeping, eating, using a
or resting, and don't allow your dog to harass your cats at any time.

ide vertical spaces—window perches, secure cat trees, and so on. The more ca
, the more use they will make of vertical spaces, and if you don't provide "leg
, they'll clear books, plants, and knickknacks from the ones they find.

ide scheduled individual meals, or if you free feed, several feeding stations. (!
ter 5.)

ide water in several places around the house.

How Much Can One Cat Sleep?

Cats definitely know the value of a good nap. In fact, although there are individual variations, most normal, healthy cats sleep about 16 hours a day—twice the length of time most mammals sleep. Sleeping cats also exhibit brain-wave patterns and body movements similar to our own during deep, dreamy sleep, suggesting that they dream. Changes in sleep habits can signal health problems, especially in senior cats, so if any of your cats seem to sleep more or fewer hours than usual, talk to your veterinarian.

heart rate and breathing speed up to prepare his body to fight or flee. His hair follicles contract and his hair stands on end to make him look bigger to an enemy. His mind also reacts—he becomes highly alert.

Fear Responses

Cats, like most animals, typically show any of four responses to fear. If you have ever tried to touch or hold a frightened cat, you know that he may react aggressively toward anyone or anything foolish enough to get in his way. That defensive aggression is the fight response. After you let him go, he runs as far as possible from the threat, exhibiting the flight response. When he stops running, he crouches and lies still, using the freeze response to avoid attention from a potential attacker. (There is a fourth possible response, appeasement, which involves submitting to the attacker, but cats rarely try to appease their enemies.)

In the wild, these responses can save an animal's life, and when the threat is gone, the mind and body return to their normal states. But when your cat cannot identify, avoid, or eliminate a threat through the normal responses (fight, flight, freeze), his fear will turn into chronic anxiety and will result in behaviors that most people find unacceptable.

Common Sources of Stress

From our perspective, our pets live a pretty cushy life. But if you live with cats, it's essential to see things through their eyes to prevent or address stress-induced behavior problems. Here are some common sources of feline stress:

- change in the environment (anything from rearranging furniture to getting a new litter box)
- change in routine
- loud noises
- unusual or strong scents and odors (from strange people, animals, potpourri, and so on)
- dirty litter box (which, for some cats, means that it's been used even once since the last cleaning)

A household with several cats can be a happy home, but increased numbers can stress them.

- changes in the litter box and/or litter
- a newcomer or guest in the house (animal or human)
- disappearance of someone from the household (animal or human)
- angry or aggressive behavior by other members of the household (animal or human)
- illness or injury to the cat himself
- illness, injury, or death of another member of the household (animal or human)
- boredom, because cats are highly intelligent, and their minds and bodies need exercise

How to Alleviate Stress

In a multi-cat household, stress is contagious. If one of your cats suffers

Purring

Purring is the quintessential feline behavior. We think of purring as a sign of contentment, and it often is. Queens (female cats) and kittens purr while nursing, and most cats purr when they are relaxed. Adult cats often purr to signal friendliness to other cats. But cats who are sick, injured, or under stress often purr as well. Behaviorists speculate that purring in such situations may be a reaction similar to nervous laughter in people under stress. It may also be a technique cats use to calm themselves when nervous.

Spaying or neutering your cats will remove any chance of them having kittens. It will also save you from the ordeal of finding responsible homes, which is more difficult than you may think.

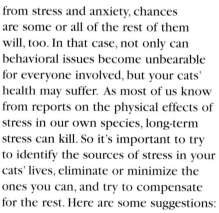

from stress and anxiety, chances are some or all of the rest of them will, too. In that case, not only can behavioral issues become unbearable for everyone involved, but your cats' health may suffer. As most of us know from reports on the physical effects of stress in our own species, long-term stress can kill. So it's important to try to identify the sources of stress in your cats' lives, eliminate or minimize the ones you can, and try to compensate for the rest. Here are some suggestions:

- Separate cats who don't get along and try reintroducing them. (See Chapter 4.)

- Give your cats things to watch. Window perches, for instance, can provide hours of entertainment.

- If you have a lot of cats, try separating them into smaller groups that occupy different parts of the house for a while. Then try reintroducing them to one another.

- People tend to see the space in a room in terms of the horizontal plane of the floor and the furniture sitting on it. To get away from each other, we move to a different part of the room. Cats see the room as a cube in which they can move up and down as well as across the floor, and they tend to organize themselves in three dimensions. One may curl up on the couch, another 5 feet (1.5 m) east of him on a chair, and a third 4 feet (about 1 m) above the chair on a shelf. You can reduce your cats' sense of being crowded by providing more secure, elevated surfaces, such as cat trees, shelves, and perches. (That will also enable your cats to get away from dogs and toddlers without hiding under the bed.)

- Ask your vet about spray products like Feliway, which contain a synthetic copy of the feline hormones that cats use to mark by rubbing their faces on things. The scent seems to calm them and may help your cats to relax, depending on the source of their stress.

Litter Prevention

When you take responsibility for an animal's well-being, you also become responsible for any and all possible offspring. That means that every litter of kittens should be carefully planned, and the kittens should be socialized, properly fed, vaccinated, wormed, examined by a vet, and carefully placed into responsible homes. It also means that you will keep any kittens you can't place, for life if necessary.

Why Spay or Neuter?

Unless you are engaged in a serious, well-planned breeding program to produce healthy cats whom you will place in responsible homes or keep or take back if necessary, there's really no good reason to leave your cats' reproductive equipment intact. There are, however, many excellent reasons to have your cats altered (spayed or neutered). Here are a few of them:

- Altered cats make better pets because they are not driven to procreate.
- Intact toms (males) mark their territories by spraying walls,

Spaying and Neutering

"Spay" (past tense "spayed," not "spade" or "spaded") is the common term for an ovariohysterectomy, the surgical sterilization of a female animal by removing her uterus and ovaries. "Neuter" is the common term for castration of a male animal. Several methods of castration are used on cats. Spayed and neutered animals of both sexes are said to be "altered." Unaltered animals are "intact."

furniture, shrubs, and so on with urine, which, although presumably pleasing to cats, is not so pleasing to most people. Neutered males are much less likely to spray.

- Intact males wander in search of love, putting them at serious risk of injury or death from fights with other tomcats, motor vehicles, and other hazards of life on the road.
- Intact queens (females) sometimes spray urine, and when they are in heat, they yowl loudly and nonstop as they yearn for love. Heats can occur as often as every other week for seven to ten days at a time.
- Intact queens attract every intact

Your Social Cats

tom for miles around to your door—think unruly biker boys spraying, brawling, and singing loudly in your yard.

- Unless you keep them locked in an impenetrable vault, intact queens become pregnant. Frequently.

- Spaying your female cats before their first heats eliminates their risk for uterine or ovarian cancers, as well as for pyometra, a potentially life-threatening infection of the uterus. Early spaying also significantly reduces their risk for mammary cancer.

- Altering eliminates your male cats' risk for testicular cancer.

Ideally, females should be spayed before they experience their first heat, which can occur as early as five months. Male kittens should be neutered no later than six months but before their urine takes on the strong odor of an intact tom and they start spraying.

Because of the horrifying number of homeless cats, many shelters, breeders, and rescuers will not release adopted kittens or cats until they have been altered. Early altering can be done safely on kittens as young as seven weeks of age. The cost of spaying and neutering varies, depending on where you live, and the individual veterinarian. If money is an issue, speak to your vet or local shelter—many communities offer free or low-cost programs.

Help Your Cats Live Their Nine Lives

Knowing how your cats see the world will make your time with them more interesting and fulfilling. Knowledge will also help you provide the sort of environment that will keep your cats happier and reduce the human-made stress in their lives. Lower stress translates to better behavior, better health, longer lives, and better relationships between you and your cats.

FAMILY-FRIENDLY TIP
Should You Breed a Litter for the Kids?

It's time, you think, for your children to learn about the miracle of birth. Besides, you only want this one litter. You'll find homes for all the kittens and then you'll have your cat spayed. Why not? Before you decide to have a litter, here are some things to consider:

- 15,000 to 20,000 pets are killed in shelters in the US *every day* because they have no homes. That's some 6 to 8 million each year. More than half are cats, including many kittens.

- Although cats are generally excellent mothers, raising a litter responsibly still requires your time for socializing the kittens, keeping their litter box and quarters clean, taking them to the vet for shots and exams, and interviewing prospective adopters.

- Raising a litter requires some financial investment—at minimum, kittens and mother cats need food, litter, and vaccinations, and you need cleaning supplies.

If you really want to have the experience of raising kittens, why not volunteer to raise a litter for a shelter or rescue program that has had a pregnant cat dumped on them? Your children will learn not only about the miracle of birth but also about the complex responsibilities of caring for another living being.

Chapter 4

Just One More—
Introducing a Newcomer

Whether you bring home a baby kitten or a mature adult, some advance planning and caution will help make everyone involved more comfortable.

Introducing a Kitten

If you haven't raised a kitten in some time, you've probably gotten used to living with cats who know the routine and have some experience and common sense. Remember, kittens are babies. They are tiny, fragile, and inexperienced but quick and daring. They can be injured or killed faster than you can say "scat."

Kitten-Proofing Your Home

Kitten-proof your home to protect your kitten and your breakables. Remove dangly decorations, including tablecloths and cords—they practically shout "Grab me!" to a playful kitten. Put toxic substances out of reach. (See Chapter 8.) Keep doors and containers closed. Encourage children and other household members to put away toys and other things that might attract a curious kitten. If you have a dog, supervise all interaction between the dog and the kitten. Even the sweetest pooch can hurt a small kitten by accident.

The same goes for children. Teach older children to handle the kitten gently. A responsible adult who is in a position to intervene immediately should supervise all interaction between preschoolers and kittens. Don't leave your kitten alone with your older cats, either, unless you are confident that they won't hurt him and that he won't pester them more than they can stand, especially if any of them are elderly or ill.

When to Bring Your Kitten Home

When should your kitten come home? Although many kittens are advertised as "ready to go" at six to eight weeks, kittens who are removed from their mothers and siblings too early may display emotional and behavioral problems that affect their relations with other creatures and even their physical health and longevity. Unfortunately, some of these problems—skittishness around strangers, excessive kneading with the paws, excessive vocalization, separation anxiety, and so on—have come to be perceived by owners as normal

Introductions between your pets and a kitten—and your children and a kitten—must be monitored closely.

behavior for cats. Sometimes the decision to take the kitten from his mom has already made by the time you meet him, but let's look at the ideal situation and what you can do to compensate if necessary.

Feline behaviorists and many serious cat breeders believe that a kitten will develop into a healthier adult, both physically and mentally, if he remains with his mother and littermates for 12 to 16 weeks. Left to their own devices, mother cats wean their kittens gradually, teaching them not only to eat solid food but also to overcome frustration as the milk bar is open fewer hours. They rely less and less on their mother until they are fully and confidently independent. Between 6 and 12 weeks of age, kittens also develop critical social skills. They learn that no one likes to be bitten and scratched and that if they play too rough, mom and siblings bite back or quit playing. Kittens learn good potty habits from their mothers, too, though many kittens don't use the litter box consistently until they are eight weeks old.

Kittens do not have fully functional immune systems until sometime between their 8th and 12th weeks. As newborns, they acquired some immunity from antibodies in their mother's milk, but it begins to wear off at around two months. Although well-cared-for kittens are generally vaccinated at around 6, 9, and 12 weeks of age, the vaccines may not take effect for up to ten days, and some studies suggest that some kittens do

FAMILY-FRIENDLY TIP

Kids and a New Cat

Most kids are thrilled when a new pet comes home and find it hard to suppress their excitement. But most cats are not thrilled by noisy, bouncing young humans, especially in an environment that's new and strange. When you bring home a new cat, be sure that he has a place to get away from kids as well as resident pets. Explain to your children that the new kitty may be frightened and that he needs a few days to get used to things. If the cat is willing, let your children spend some time quietly interacting with him with adult supervision. Don't overstress the newcomer—let him set the pace. In a short time, he'll probably be playing chase the paper ball and snuggling with your kids.

not develop lasting immunity from vaccines given earlier than 16 weeks of age. During this in-between time, they are highly susceptible to disease. (See Chapter 7.)

Does this mean that you should never adopt a young kitten who needs a home? Not at all. But if you do adopt a very young kitten into your feline family, being aware of the potential problems may help you help your kitten avoid them. If your current cats are good with kittens, they will teach him a lot.

Introducing Adult Cats to One Another

Even if your cats are used to living with other cats, they may not be amused if you bring home another feline friend for them. The newcomer, too, may be less than delighted to find one or more other cats in this strange new place. How long it will take everyone to adjust depends on their ages, social skills, individual personalities, and how low-stress you can make the introductory period. Some cats are quite blasé about new family members; others stay in a snit for months. The best thing you can do is to keep control of the situation, provide for each cat's security and privacy, and give them time to adjust without forcing the issue.

On Their Own Terms

Both the resident cat or cats and the newcomer will adapt more easily if you let them adjust to one another's presence in the house without direct contact at first. Confine your new cat to a room with a closed door. Let him get to know the smells and sounds of his new home. Spend some time interacting with him, but let the cat set the pace. If he's a big cuddle bug and climbs purring into your lap, that's great. If he prefers to peer at you from under the bed or the top of the bookcase, that's okay too. Each human member of the family should spend some time in the "cat room," but don't overwhelm the newcomer with too many people at once. If you have kids, explain that the new kitty needs time to get used to everyone, and encourage them to be calm and reasonably quiet when near him for a while.

Scent Introductions

You can facilitate scent introductions in a number of ways. At first, make the

Names for Housemates

Finding the perfect name for each of your cats can be a challenge. Some cats look at you and seem to say "Hi! My name is Leo." Others are more circumspect about their names and expect you to take some time to figure them out.

Choose names that sound distinct from one another. Calling your cats Bill, Phil, and Jill may seem cute at first but will make it difficult for each cat to recognize his or her own name. Names should also sound distinct from any commands you might use. If "Off!" means "vacate the kitchen counter," don't name your cats "Puff" and "Jeff." Short names are easier for you to say and for your cat to learn than long ones—"Alakazam" may be fun, but "Presto" is more practical. Remember, too, that kittens turn into cats. They should have names that will still suit them when they're grown up.

At a loss for name ideas? Here are some places to look:

- If you want a name to reflect a color, check out names of paint colors in an art or paint store, or look at lists of flowers or minerals or other things you like.

- If you believe, as many people do, that your cats have mystical powers, check out lists of mythical beings from different cultures.

- Baby name books and websites list thousands of names from all languages.

- Visit 2000 Cat Names at www.petrix.com/catnames.

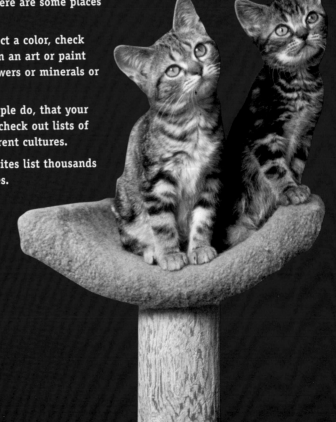

SENIOR CAT TIP

Adopting a Senior

Wonderful older adult cats are available for adoption through shelters and rescue organizations. Many people are reluctant to adopt them, commonly citing fears that an older cat won't bond to them and won't live as long as a younger one. Having adopted several older cats, I can tell you that they can and do adjust to new situations and bond with new people and pets. As far as longevity goes, the fact is that there are no guarantees. Some cats live into their twenties, while some die very young. The only way to spare ourselves the sorrow of losing a cat is to deny ourselves the magic and pleasure of ever living with cats. When you adopt an older cat, you get exactly what you see, with the added bonus of knowing that he needs you as much as you need him.

the newcomer and your other cats. Rub a towel over your new cat or hold him wrapped in one for a few minutes, and then put the towel where your other cats can smell it. Rub another towel over your resident cats, or take a rug or cushions that they lie on and put them in the room with your new cat. The cats will be able to investigate the scents at leisure without the stress of direct contact. You might place the cats' food bowls or some special treats on the scented materials—associating food with the other cats' scents can be a terrific icebreaker. They can also sniff each other under the door but won't be able to see each other, so any aggressive displays on either side will be audio only. They may hiss and growl at first, but that should stop in a few days.

Trading Places

Once your new cat relaxes a bit in his room, it's time to have the cats trade places. Don't allow any direct contact yet. If you have carriers for everyone,

cat room one that your other cats have been in. Keep the door closed so that there is no direct interaction between

you can prevent accidental encounters by putting all the cats in carriers and then switching them around. Close the door, and then let your resident cat or cats loose in the room while your new cat explores the rest of the house for a few hours. Show him where the litter boxes are, and be sure that there's a nice clean one for him to use. After a few hours, return the cats to their original spaces.

Meet Your New Feline Family

When the cats relax a bit, you can let them see each other but still without full contact. If you have more than one resident cat, introduce each one individually to the new guy, and give him a break between introductions. There are several good ways to introduce the cats. You can put both cats in carriers and set the carriers door to door, allowing them to see and smell and hear each other but preventing physical contact. Or you can put one of them in a carrier and let the other be loose in the same room. You can also prop open the door to the cat room just enough to let the cats see one another and poke paws through.

When the cats adjust to seeing each other, begin feeding them in sight of one another. If that goes well, try feeding them at opposite sides of a room with no barrier between. Don't leave them alone yet, and when they finish eating, separate them again. Slowly, over the course of a few days, move the food dishes closer together until they are eating side by side. If

Most cats will eventually tolerate one another's company.

Whiskers

One of the most distinctive features of a cat's face is his whiskers, or vibrissae. But whiskers are more than a fashion statement. These specialized hairs are linked to very sensitive nerves that send complex messages to the brain as the cat senses his environment. Nor are whiskers limited to the face; your cats' carpal vibrissae, located on their front legs, help them sense prey that they capture and grasp in their paws. Take a close look at your cats and you'll see that their whiskers are arranged in distinctive patterns. In fact, every cat's whisker pattern is as unique as every person's fingerprints.

you have multiple cats, you'll need to repeat the process until everyone can "sit down" to family meals together.

Now that the cats associate one another with good things, let them have access to each other when a responsible adult is present. Don't leave them alone together until you're sure that they get along, but if they seem compatible at this point, it won't be long until you can curtail the supervision.

If any of your cats acts frightened or aggressive at any step in this process, just back up and go more slowly. Each cat's individual personality and history will affect how he adjusts to the new living arrangements.

Meet Fido

Cats and dogs can certainly live in peace, and many develop strong friendships. Ideally, kittens and puppies have positive encounters with the other species while they are young and impressionable. But even cats who have not grown up with dogs can learn

to accept dogs and maybe even like them. Whether you are introducing a new cat into your family of cats and at least one dog or introducing a dog into your family of cats, you are more likely to be successful if you are patient and keep control of the situation.

If you are bringing in a new cat, follow the same procedures you would for introducing the new cat to the resident cats. Let the cat explore and sniff where the dogs have been when the dogs are out. When it comes time for face-to-face introductions, limit the initial encounter to just the new cat and the dog (one at a time if you have multiple dogs). If you are bringing in a new dog, introduce him to each cat individually.

I have also had great success with initial encounters by confining the dog to a crate for short periods and allowing the cat or cats to get used to the canine presence on the cat's own terms, then separating them again until everyone is relaxed. If the cats want to get a close look at the dog, that's great, but let the cats determine how quickly the relationship will develop. Talk to both the cat and the dog to help them understand that they both belong in the family now. Don't punish the cats if they hiss or swipe at the dog—they need to set the limits. Keep the dog under control, on leash if necessary. If one or more of your cats are really upset, separate them and try again later.

Be sure that you give your cats dog-free zones where they can sleep, eat, play, and use the litter boxes without canine involvement. Don't allow the dog or dogs to chase cats—*not ever.* Regardless of whether the newcomer is the cat or the dog, a responsible adult should monitor all interaction among your pets until you're sure they get along together. Don't take chances. A dog can kill or seriously injure a cat, sometimes intentionally and sometimes by accident. A cat can also seriously injure a dog. If you see any sign of aggression or if either plays too roughly, separate them and try again later.

Cats and Other Pets

We've all seen photos of cats and hamsters or parakeets cuddled up together. Such friendships are certainly possible, but cats must learn, usually as kittens, to regard small prey-type pets as family, not food. In fact, if your cats are not exposed to such little creatures repeatedly and under controlled conditions when the cats are between two and seven weeks old, they will probably never form close bonds with

Cats and dogs who have known each other from kittenhood and puppyhood can form a close bond later in life.

small mammals and birds. The feline predatory instinct is just too strong.

It's up to you, then, to protect any small pets in your family from your cats. Even if you socialize your kittens to small animals, it's always possible for your cats' hunting instincts to be triggered, so never leave cats and small pets alone together. The safety of your parakeets and gerbils is your responsibility. It's unrealistic and unfair to expect your cats to resist their natural impulses under all circumstances.

Keep vulnerable pets in secure enclosures with paw-proof latches on the doors, and if possible, keep your cats out of the room where the little guys live unless you are present. Put birdcages out of reach, make sure that doors are securely latched, and provide hiding places in small pets' enclosures. Knowing that they're being watched by predators is extremely stressful for your little furry creatures. Explain to your children that it's simply a cat's nature to hunt things. Remind them to latch cages, but be sure that an adult makes a security check from time to time to prevent a tragedy.

roducing a new cat to resident pets, safety should always come first. Accidents are
sy when animals become excited or fearful, especially when they are still strangers
other. Make careful introductions as outlined in this chapter. Here are some other
can take to minimize the risk of injuries:

our cats' claws.

too, should have a nail trim.

logs on leashes during introductions and until you are confident about their
ior, and obedience train your dogs so that you have at least some voice control.

mall animals and birds in secure cages and out of reach of the cats.

e that the cats have an escape path and secure, private places to go if they want to
ay.

force things—let the animals negotiate their relationships at their own pace.

Chapter 5

Feeding Multiple Cats

Choosing the right foods for your family of cats can be quite the challenge. Should you buy your cats' food from your vet, from a pet-supply store, or on sale at the local supermarket? Should you dish it up from bags or cans? Should you cook it yourself? And what can you do if one of your cats likes his grub a bit too much or not enough? So many questions over so basic a part of life! Let's sniff out a few answers.

Nutrients for a Balanced Feline Diet

Cats are carnivores. Their teeth are designed for shearing meat, not for chewing vegetation, and their digestive systems are designed to process meat proteins efficiently. Cats do need some vegetable matter in their diets, but they cannot digest it without some help. In the wild, the partially digested contents of prey animals provide usable vegetable nutrients. For domestic cats, cooking breaks down cellulose so that the nutrients in vegetables can be utilized. This is the case whether you feed your cats commercial foods or home-cooked meals.

Food comprises the following nutrients:

- *Proteins*, made up of amino acids, are highly concentrated in meats, fish, poultry, milk, cheese, yogurt, eggs, soybeans, and dehydrated plant extracts. Cats generally need a high percentage of protein for good health, but each individual's needs depend on his age, size, activity level, and health status.

- *Dietary fat* is found in rich supply in meats, milk, butter, and vegetable oils. It provides energy, cushions internal organs, insulates against cold, helps transport nutrients to the organs, and makes food more palatable. Fat is cheaper than protein, and most lower-quality commercial foods are high in fat. In the proper amounts, dietary fat promotes good health, but a high-fat diet often lacks the protein, vitamins, and minerals essential to long-term health.

- *Vitamins* are chemical compounds that promote good health in many ways. Vitamins can be destroyed by light, heat, moisture, and rancidity, so food should be stored properly and used before its expiration date.

- *Minerals* build and strengthen bones and cell tissue and help organs function properly.

- *Water* is vital to sound nutrition. Your cats should have access to clean water at all times, and with multiple cats, you may need to provide several water bowls in different locations to ensure that each cat has easy access.

A basic knowledge of feline nutrition is a great start, but the real measure of the diet you offer your feline family is each cat's appearance

Buy your cats the best-quality food you can afford. Skimping here will negatively affect their health and life spans.

and health. If each of your cats has a sleek, healthy skin and coat, is well covered with flesh without being fat, and is active and alert as suits his age, then he's probably eating the right things in the right amounts. If one seems not to be doing well on the household diet, speak to your vet. A medical problem could be at fault, or he may need a different diet.

What's for Dinner?

When it comes to choosing food for our cats, the sheer variety of available foods is almost overwhelming. There seems to be a food for every variation of felineness you can think of except—for now!—coat color. Does that mean that if you have four cats of different ages you need four different foods? In most cases, no. Unless one or more of your cats need a special diet because of a health problem, chances are all your cats will do fine on the same foods. Let's look at the basic options.

Commercial Cat Foods

Commercial cat foods come in a wide variety of formulas using a wide variety of ingredients presented in dry, semi-moist, and canned. The most expensive commercial foods aren't always the best—in fact, some of the best-known brands spend enormous amounts of money on advertisements that are fun to look at but do nothing to enhance your cats' diet. Cheap foods, on the other hand, use cheap ingredients that don't promote health and may actually harm your cats. Food dyes and other ingredients in low-quality cat foods have been linked to allergies and other health and behavior problems.

As the recent tragic deaths of a number of pets have taught us, the convenience of commercial cat foods

FAMILY-FRIENDLY TIP

Kids Feeding Cats

In theory, putting kids in charge of pet care sounds like a great way to teach them to be nurturing and responsible. In the real world, children lack experience and judgment, and they sometimes simply forget. An adult must see that your cats are fed and cared for properly.

sometimes comes with a price. If you love your cats, it's worth a little extra time and effort to research what goes into any cat food you plan to give them. There are foods on the market that use human-grade ingredients from reliable sources and no fillers, dyes, or hazardous preservatives.

Commercial cat foods typically come in three forms: dry, semi-moist, and canned.

Dry

Dry food, also known as kibble, is easy to store and feed. Dry food also tends to produce firmer stools, making litter box cleanup easier—not a minor factor when you have more than one cat. Although sacrificing quality nutrients to cost is false economy (you'll end

up giving your vet whatever you save buying cheap food), the expense of feeding several cats may be a factor, and dry food usually costs less than canned foods of equal quality. So for many multi-cat households, dry food is the best option.

Semi-Moist

Semi-moist foods are essentially kibble in a soft form. They are usually more expensive than kibble, and many contain dyes to make them look better to people. Your cats, though, don't care what color their food is. Many semi-moist foods also contain preservatives that have been linked to health and behavior problems.

Canned

Canned cat foods are comparatively expensive, mostly to pay for the can and the water inside. For cats with certain medical conditions, particularly those who need to consume more water, high-quality canned foods may be a good choice. On the negative side, a diet of mostly canned food often causes tartar buildup, flatulence, bad breath, and soft, smelly stools. Canned food also spoils quickly and attracts insects and rodents (which you really don't want your cats fooling with, even though they will), so dishes need to be washed promptly and thoroughly after each meal. Canned foods are nice for an occasional treat but may not be the best choice for most multi-cat homes.

Homemade Cat Foods

If, like many people, you feel less than confident about the safety and nutritional value of commercial foods (although good ones are available), you may prefer to make your cats' food yourself so that you know what they are eating. Before you pounce on the homemade idea, though, be sure that you understand the challenges as well as the advantages of making your cats' food.

Shopping for ingredients and preparing food takes time, of course. You need room to store the ingredients safely, which means refrigeration for meats, dairy products, and vegetables, and air-tight, vermin-proof containers for other ingredients. If you feed a cooked diet, you need to set aside time to prepare, cook, and cool the food at least every few days and time to warm it before serving if it's refrigerated. If you feed a raw diet, you will still need time to prepare and assemble the ingredients and to process the vegetables. Sanitation can also be an issue, especially when you are dealing

SENIOR CAT TIP

Food for Seniors

Do your senior cats need a special senior cat food? Probably not. Unless they have medical problems that require special diets, a high-quality maintenance food should provide everything your older cats need.

with raw meats that can harbor bacteria and parasites that can make you and your cats ill.

If you decide that you can handle the challenges of preparing your cats' food, base their diet on reliable information about feline nutrition. Advice on homemade diets is easy to come by these days, especially on the Internet. Be careful—anyone can post unfounded opinions, and a lot of "information" out there is inaccurate. Your cats need to consume a

51

Feeding Multiple Cats

Some cats may be able to eat peacefully from the same dish at the same time, while others may need to be fed from separate bowls. Still others may need to be fed in separate rooms.

balanced, complete diet that provides the nutrients necessary for good health, so do your homework to ensure that your good intentions have the result you want.

Managing Mealtimes

Feeding more than one cat can provide some challenges, but there's no reason for mealtimes to become chaotic or overly difficult. Let's see how you can make meals run smoothly.

Free Feeding Versus Scheduled Feeding

Many people who feed their cats dry foods leave food down all the time. If all of your cats eat the same food and none of them have weight problems,

free feeding may be a good option for you and your feline family. But suppose your cats vary in their food needs. Perhaps one is pudgy, another needs a special diet for health reasons, and a third likes to guard the food and keep the others from eating. With such variables, scheduled feedings make sense.

One good reason to feed your cats scheduled meals is that you can control how much food each gets, enabling you to prevent or deal with obesity in one or more of your cats. People assume all too often that cats won't overeat if they can free feed, but that just isn't true. If your cat begins to put on excess weight, it almost always means that he's eating too much. (In rare cases a medical problem may be at fault, but that's very unusual.) Scheduled feedings work best, too, if one or more of your cats need a special diet for health reasons.

Even if your cats all eat the same foods, scheduled meals are a good idea for a number of reasons. Mealtimes help reinforce your bond with your cats because you dole out the food. Scheduled meals alert you right away if one of your cats stops eating. Because loss of appetite often signals a serious health problem, the sooner you know, the sooner you can get veterinary help for your cat. If you simply put food out and let them all have at it, you may not notice for some time if one of them stops eating.

If you have been free feeding your cats and decide to switch to scheduled meals, you can expect a little confusion

How to Change Your Cat's Food

From time to time you may decide to change the food that one or all of your cats eat. Perhaps someone needs a special food because of a health issue, or you've decided to switch to a new brand, formula, or type of food. The change may be good, but introducing a new food suddenly can cause vomiting or diarrhea in some cats. Older cats and cats who have eaten the same food for most of their lives seem to be particularly vulnerable to upset stomachs. However, you can ease them into the switch by mixing the new food into the old. Start small and gradually increase the proportion of new food and decrease the proportion of old over the course of a week or two. Your cats should adjust with few problems.

Kitty Treats

If, like most cat owners, you like to give your cats a treat now and then, use the same criteria you would for choosing their regular food. Find treats that are nutritionally sound and that don't contain dyes and other chemicals. If any of your cats has allergies or other food-related health issues, remember that treats can cause problems just like regular food. Finally, don't overdo it. Too many treats can throw your cats' diets off and pack on extra weight.

for a day or two. You'll probably hear some complaints, too, because cats aren't usually happy about changes in their routines. Still, no matter what they may think, you're in charge!

How to Switch From Free Feeding to Scheduled Feeding

Decide on a day to begin scheduled feeding, and figure out how many meals you plan to offer. Two—breakfast and dinner—work well for most people and (once they adjust) most cats. Decide also whether you will feed all your cats in one place or separate them. If you need to ensure that individuals eat specific foods, you have to feed them in different places—you might feed them in separate rooms. A friend of mine feeds each of her five cats in his or her own carrier. They run to their private "dining rooms" when she starts dishing up meals!

You will also need to determine serving sizes for each of your cats. It may be hit and miss at first, but you can adjust the servings as you observe how each maintains weight and energy on his new rations. If you feed commercial food or use a recipe that includes portion sizes, keep in mind that every animal's needs are different. Portion sizes are usually given in ranges based on the cat's size and age, but they are only general guidelines. You need to keep an eye on each of your cats and adjust their daily portions according to their individual needs.

The night before the first day of the new regime, pick up all the food you have out. When the first scheduled mealtime arrives, put the food down for up to half an hour. If you have more than one cat, supervise the first few meals to make sure that things go smoothly, and do the same off and on after that. If one is a fast eater and wants to "help" with another's food, separate them as described in the first paragraph of this section.

Fat Cats

Funny photos of lazy fat cats lounging in goofy positions aside, excess weight is as bad for felines as it is for humans. Obesity contributes to many serious health problems and can shorten your cat's life, and except in very rare cases, fat comes from too much food. Each of your cats has different needs based on:

- *Activity level.* Cats who play and run around need more food than do couch potatoes.
- *Quality of food.* The more nutritionally dense their food, the less your cats need to eat.
- *Individual variation.* As you already know, every cat is an individual, and that individuality applies just as much to nutritional needs as it does to looks and personality.

Cats who live with other cats are more likely to stay active than single cats, and active cats are more likely to remain at their proper weights. Still, an occasional cat turns into a piggy when he thinks there's competition for food, and some individuals are just more prone to packing on an extra pound or two (about half to 1 kg). That may not sound like much, but for a 10-pound (4.5-kg) animal, 2 extra pounds (about 1 kg) is like an extra 24 pounds (11 kg) on a 120-pound (54-kg) person. If any of your cats gains (or loses) weight, adjust his daily rations. If you are free feeding, put everyone on scheduled meals so that you can control what each one eats. If you don't see an improvement in a couple of weeks, speak to your vet (especially if your cat is losing weight or muscle tone).

Finicky Felines

Your cats may never have to catch their own meals, but they nevertheless retain the predatory senses of their wild heritage. In fact, with the exception of the sense of taste, your cats have sensory organs more finely tuned

Obesity in cats is a serious health concern.

than yours. The average person has 18 times as many taste buds as does the average cat, but your cats can sniff circles around you. Cats live in a world rich in scent, and their noses make fine distinctions that help them communicate with other cats, sense danger, navigate, and find prey. If you watch your cats' expressions as they sniff things, it's clear that they find some odors offensive and some pleasurable. It figures, then, that your cats rely more on fragrance than on taste to decide whether they like certain foods.

Some cats are fussier than others about what they will eat. Lack of appetite, especially if it's a new behavior in a particular cat, can indicate a health problem (see Chapter 7), so if one of your cats stops eating or declines to eat despite your efforts to encourage him, get him a checkup. But many cats who are finicky about their food will perk up if the food becomes more fragrant. This is particularly true of older cats because their senses, including the sense of smell, become less keen as they age.

To encourage a finicky kitty with no health problems to eat, try making his food more fragrant. Moisture helps scent to move in the air, so if you feed dry cat food, pour a little warm water or salt-free broth over the serving and let it sit for about five minutes. If you feed canned or frozen food, you can make it smell better (to your cats, at least!) by warming it slightly. Just be sure that it's not hot enough to burn anyone when you serve it.

He Touched My Food!

In any family, squabbles occasionally break out, and food can trigger conflict from time to time. It may be that one of your cats thinks he owns *all* the food and can tell the others to bug off. Or it may be that two of your cats aren't overly fond of one another in any circumstances, and dislike comes to blows when both want to eat from the same bowl at the same time. Whatever

the source of the conflict, fights over meals don't help anyone's digestion.

What can you do? The simplest solution is to feed your cats scheduled meals, separating them as described earlier. If you prefer to free feed your cats, adding an extra feeding station or two in different parts of the house may help keep the peace because individuals can choose not only when to eat, but where.

Give the Best to Your Feline Companions

High-quality food and a well-planned approach to mealtimes work together to promote good health and harmony in your multi-cat home.

Chapter 6

Behave Yourselves!

Some feline behaviors that you dislike may be perfectly normal from a cat's-eye view. Your job is to provide an environment that encourages behaviors you approve and discourages the rest so that you can live in harmony with your cats. When one or more of your cats do things you find intolerable, it's up to you to figure out why the behavior is occurring and what you can do about it.

We don't have room to cover every behavior issue that you could encounter, but the same principles apply to managing most undesirable behaviors. First, rule out illness or injury. Then, review "Stress in Your Multi-Cat Home" in Chapter 3. Try to identify the cause of the behavior, remove it if possible, give your cats an alternative, and train them to do what you want them to do. If you don't see improvement quickly, seek professional help.

What Is Training?

Training is the process of creating behavior patterns in which a specific stimulus (a command or a need, such as the urge to scratch) results in a specific response. Training can also be a process of retraining, during which a previously learned response is replaced by a different one that the trainer prefers. Most cat training is actually retraining, or problem solving. But there's no reason to wait for problems to develop. One of the best reasons to train a pet is to prevent unwanted behaviors before they begin.

Consistency is a vital element of teaching your cats and preventing problem behaviors. Everyone in your household needs to permit and discourage the same behaviors. If you don't allow your cats to nap on the dining room table and someone else pets them when they're lounging there, the cats won't know whether they should be there or not.

In the remainder of this chapter, we'll explore training to manage specific behaviors.

If you do not provide "legal" scratching or play areas for your cats, you may find them getting into things you don't want them in!

Common Behavior Problems

House Soiling

Inappropriate elimination is the most common behavior problem reported in pet cats. Soiling can take many forms, but typically the cat deposits urine or feces, but not both, outside the box some or all of the time. It's not uncommon for cats who have always had reliable toilet habits to suddenly begin soiling in the house. Quick action to fix this is essential.

Before you do anything else, you need to determine which of your cats is soiling. If you're not sure, ask your veterinarian for an edible dye that will color urine. Give it to one cat at a time until you identify the offender. Then get that cat a complete checkup to make sure that he doesn't have a medical problem.

Once you know which cat is soiling and you eliminate any health issues, it's time to look for other causes. Common triggers for changes in potty habits among cats who live with other cats include the following:

- Litter-box crowding: As noted earlier, you need one more box than you have cats. Some cats just don't like litter boxes that get too much traffic.

- The litter box: Some cats dislike boxes with covers. Elderly cats, very small kittens, and cats with orthopedic problems may find boxes with high sides too difficult to manage. Cats will also avoid boxes that are too small—they

No Pine Oil, Please

Pine oil is toxic to cats (and many other animals). *Do not* use cleaners or fragrances containing pine oil on litter boxes or other areas accessible to your cats.

should be able to turn around, squat, and dig comfortably.

- The litter: If your cats vary in their litter preferences, you need to use two or three different types of litter in different boxes to give everyone a choice. Cats also vary in how much litter they like. Some like it deep, others shallow. Some cats don't like any litter at all. If one of your cats is using smooth surfaces (floors, bathtubs), an empty litter box may fix the problem.

- Strong scents: Scented litter, residual odors from cleaners, and even strong scents near the box (such as perfumed air fresheners) may drive cats away.

- Liners: Plastic liners can snag digging claws, and some cats just won't use a box with a liner in it.

- Location: Litter boxes should not be placed near your cats' food or water, and it should be off-limits to dogs and away from household traffic. At the same time, boxes

Behave Yourselves!

Health and Housetraining

Inappropriate elimination is sometimes the result of a medical problem, especially in elderly cats. If urination or defecation causes pain, cats may associate the pain with the litter box and look for other places to go. Some of the health problems that can cause house soiling include:

- feline lower urinary tract disease (FLUTD)
- kidney or liver disease
- colitis or inflammatory bowel disease
- inflamed or impacted anal sac
- diabetes mellitus
- hyperthyroidism
- arthritis
- vision problems

If one of your cats begins to avoid the litter boxes, tell your vet about the problem and make sure that your cat has no underlying medical problem.

should be reasonably accessible for all of your cats. If you have a senior cat who sleeps most of the time on an upstairs bed, he may have trouble toddling to a litter box in the basement.

- Cleanliness: Cats abhor dirty "bathrooms," and their definitions of dirty differ. Some don't like to share the facilities, and some prefer to urinate in one box and defecate in another.

- Traumatic experience: If something frightens your cat while he's using the litter box, he may associate the box or its location with the fear.

Identifying the reason for your cat's behavior may give you a simple solution. Here are some additional suggestions to encourage good elimination habits.

- Remove all trace of urine or feces odor from wherever your cat has gone outside the box so that your cats don't smell it and think "Go here." Surface-level urine can be neutralized with a 50–50 mix of white vinegar and water or with enzyme-based cleaners that remove organic odors. If urine has soaked through to the pad or subfloor, you may have to replace the carpet and

pad and clean and seal
the underfloor.

- After you deodorize the area, feed
your cats (or just the one who
eliminated there) on that
spot temporarily.

- If you don't want to feed your cats
on the "illegal" spot, keep them away
from it to break the habit. Close a
door, use a repellant, or make the
surface unpleasant (temporarily
cover it with plastic, aluminum foil,
double-sided sticky tape, or plastic
carpet runners placed upside-down,
spikes or nubs up).

- Confine the offending cat to a small
room or even a kitty cage with
water, bedding, toys, and litter box.
Feed him there as well. When he
uses the litter box reliably, slowly
expand his access to other parts of
the house. Be sure to spend time
with him every day. Confinement is
meant to redirect his behavior, not
to punish him.

The worst thing you can do is to
punish your cat. His behavior is not
directed at you; it's a response to some
form of stress. Hitting, yelling, and other
physical and emotional responses will
simply increase your cat's stress and
make the problem worse. You will also
lose his trust. Addressing the source of
the behavior and using positive training
will be much more productive.

Litter and the Litter Boxes

To encourage your cats to use the
proper facilities, place litter boxes
in quiet, low-traffic areas. Provide
one litter box for each of your cats
plus one. In other words, if you have
five cats, you need six litter boxes.
If possible, put them in at least two
different rooms. If that is not possible,
place them as far apart as feasible.
Make sure that the litter boxes are
inaccessible to your dog. If your cats
track litter out of the boxes, place the
boxes on washable rugs or mats that
will catch the litter.

Remove waste at least once a day.
Many cats are fussy about cleanliness
and will stop using a box that isn't up

Positive Reinforcement

If the only way your cat can get your attention is by being naughty, that's what he'll do. Why not pay attention to him for being smart and good instead? Positive reinforcement is the process of rewarding your cat with something he likes for doing what you want him to do. When your cats hear the sound of the can opening, come running, and get fed, they are getting positive reinforcement. You can use the same principle to reward your cats for scratching their posts instead of your drapes and other acceptable behaviors. Give treats for good behaviors, and train away the ones you don't like.

to their standards, especially if they are sharing the facilities. Some litters are designed to help fight odors; plain baking soda mixed into regular cat litter also works. Don't use strongly scented disinfectants or fragrances—a scent that you find pleasant may overpower your cats and chase them away from the litter boxes. Wash the boxes with hot, soapy water once or twice a week, depending on how many cats are using each one. You can disinfect the boxes with a 10 percent bleach solution (one part bleach in nine parts water), which will kill most bacteria and viruses. Rinse the boxes thoroughly to remove all trace of soap or bleach residue and scent, and dry them completely before refilling with litter.

The litter you use can also encourage or discourage your cats from using litter boxes. In fact, you may need to offer two or more different litters if your cats have different preferences. Most cats seem to like relatively fine-grained, unscented sand- or clay-based litters, but some don't. Here are the most popular litter options:

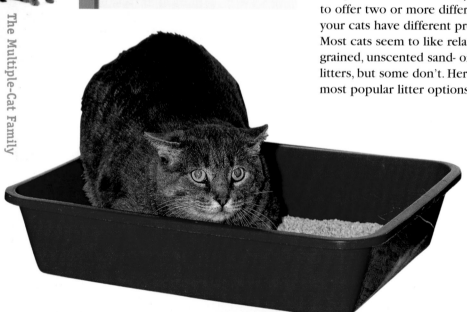

Toxoplasmosis and Pregnant Women

Toxoplasmosis, a parasitic disease, is one of the few diseases that affect both cats and people. It can cause birth defects if acquired by a pregnant woman. Cats are often blamed for transmitting toxoplasmosis, or toxo, to people, but there has never been a documented case of toxo transmission from cat to human. You are more likely to contract the disease from eating or improperly handling undercooked meat, especially pork. Cats do shed the parasite in their feces but only for a few weeks after their first exposure, and only if the feces remain in the box for at least 36 hours. The Centers for Disease Control and Prevention (CDC) estimate that about one-third of people in the US have been infected with toxoplasmosis without ever knowing it. The disease is a problem only if you are pregnant or immunosuppressed. Once you have toxoplasmosis, you become immune to it.

To protect your cats from toxoplasmosis:

Feed them dry, canned, or cooked foods—no raw meat.

Keep them indoors so that they can't hunt or eat wildlife.

Keep garbage and raw meats out of their reach.

To protect your human family from toxoplasmosis:

Cook meat thoroughly, especially pork.

If you are pregnant or plan to become pregnant, ask your doctor for a "toxo titer" to determine whether you have had toxoplasmosis. The CDC reports that a woman who tests positive for toxoplasmosis antibodies before she becomes pregnant *will not* pass the parasite to her fetus.

If you are pregnant and at risk for toxoplasmosis, do not handle raw meat.

Clean your cats' litter boxes at least once a day. Once a week, wash the boxes with soap or detergent, rinse them with scalding water, and refill them with fresh litter.

Wear gloves when cleaning litter boxes, then dispose of the gloves or wash them in hot water and detergent. Wash your hands thoroughly with soap and hot water.

If you are pregnant and at risk for toxoplasmosis, have someone else clean the litter boxes.

- Traditional clay-based litters absorb some urine but must be scooped and changed frequently.

- Clumping litters form clumps or balls when wet. In theory, you can scoop out waste and leave clean litter behind, making it unnecessary to change the litter as often. In practice, clumps often break apart. Some clumping litters are labeled as flushable (but they should *never* be flushed into septic systems). The fine dust released by clumping litters tends to get tracked around; it bothers some people and can cause intestinal blockages when cats ingest the particles during grooming.

- Farm and feed stores often carry inexpensive litters made from ground corncobs.

- Wood shavings can be used for cheap litter, but some cats won't step on them once they become wet.

- Pelletized pine litter is supposed to be dust free and nearly odorless, and it needs less frequent changes as long as waste is removed regularly.

Scent Marking (Spraying)

To most people, all cat urine smells pretty much the same—bad! But to your cats, urine carries a wealth of information, and there is an enormous difference between simply urinating to answer nature's call and spraying urine onto vertical surfaces for social reasons. (See Chapter 3.) Spraying proclaims ownership and defines

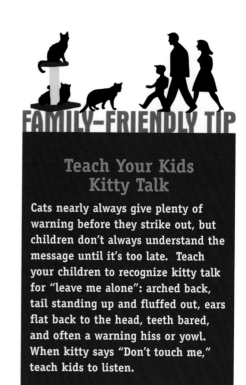

FAMILY-FRIENDLY TIP

Teach Your Kids Kitty Talk

Cats nearly always give plenty of warning before they strike out, but children don't always understand the message until it's too late. Teach your children to recognize kitty talk for "leave me alone": arched back, tail standing up and fluffed out, ears flat back to the head, teeth bared, and often a warning hiss or yowl. When kitty says "Don't touch me," teach kids to listen.

territory, and it can be a response to stress. It is most common in intact (unneutered) males and in cats who live in multi-cat environments, although unspayed females and altered (spayed or neutered) animals will sometimes engage in this behavior. Cats will also spray in response to scent marks left by other cats.

To spray, the cat backs up to a vertical surface (a tree, drapes, furniture, a wall) and squirts it with a powerful blast of urine. The cat will then "update his sites" by respraying them whenever the scent begins to dissipate.

The best cure for spraying is

prevention, and the best prevention is spaying and neutering before six months of age—that

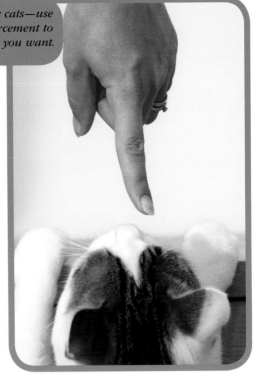

is, before the testosterone surge that urges intact male cats to claim their territories. Although it does occur, spraying is rare in cats who are neutered before they reach six months of age, even when they live with other cats.

Reducing environmental stress also reduces the urge to spray. Encourage your cats to get along so that they see one another as family members, not interlopers. Mutual grooming is a bonding activity that you can encourage by wiping each of your cats with a damp cloth in the presence of the others. Feed them together (see Chapter 5), and make play and cuddle times group activities, but also allow each cat a chance for privacy. They will be less likely to spray if they don't see each other as competition for the good things in life. Cats like routines, so try to feed them and clean their litter boxes on a regular schedule. Don't move their food, water, litter boxes, scratching posts, beds, and so on around unless absolutely necessary.

If one of your cats starts to spray, you need to act quickly to stop him before he becomes set in his ways, and you must keep your other cats from following suit. If the sprayer is not yet altered, have that taken care of immediately. Clean wherever your cat has sprayed, and if possible, keep him

Don't yell at your cats—use positive reinforcement to teach them what you want.

away from the places he likes to spray until the habit is broken.

Unfortunately, if the problem is too many cats for the space available (from their perspective, not yours), your options are limited. Talk to your vet about possible drug therapy to control spraying. As a last resort, you may need to find a new home for one or more of the cats.

Scratch Here

Cats need to scratch to keep their claws healthy. (See Chapter 7.) Outdoor cats use tree trunks and other rough objects for scratching, but if your cats are indoors, you will need to provide

67

Behave Yourselves!

Should Your Cats Be Declawed?

Onychectomy (declawing) is the amputation of the claw and surrounding tissue, sometimes including the first joint of the toe. It is a painful procedure for a cat. Most cats can be taught to use only "legal" places to scratch, such as scratching posts, making declawing unnecessary. Many veterinarians refuse to declaw, and the procedure is now illegal in some countries.

suitable substitutes. A wide variety of scratchable items are available commercially, or you can make a simple scratching station by securely fastening carpeting or several layers of burlap to a wooden post or board.

Cats have individual preferences about where and how they scratch, so you may need to provide several different options that let some of your cats stretch their bodies and front legs vertically and others horizontally. Many cats take to their scratching stations with no problem; others need a little encouragement. When your reluctant cat shows interest in the scratching post or board, reward him with a tiny treat. If you see him scratching where he shouldn't, calmly move him to the right place and encourage him to scratch there. Don't yell or throw things—frightening your cat will cause more problems than it solves. You just want to divert him from the undesirable behavior and show him what's allowed. If necessary, when you can't supervise him, put your cat in a closed room with fewer tempting surfaces other than a legal scratching

station. Be patient and persistent and he'll get the idea.

If you've provided a scratching post and encouraged your cats to use it, but one or more are still ripping up your belongings, don't despair. The solution may be simpler than you think. Here are some things to try:

- Provide different types of scratching equipment.

- Provide as many scratching stations as you have cats. Some individuals won't scratch where other cats have left their scent.

- Scatter scratching stations throughout the house, especially near your cats' favorite sleeping places. Many cats like to scratch when they wake up.

- If your cats have scratched items in your house, remove the scent that has been deposited where you don't want the cats to scratch. Clean the areas thoroughly with an enzyme product designed to remove organic scents.

- After you clean and de-scent the object, make it inaccessible to your cats until the habit is broken. You could also spray it with a product made to repel cats, but take a whiff before you buy so that you don't repel yourself, too!

Separation Anxiety

If your absence is stressful enough to make any of your cats behave badly, they could have separation anxiety. This condition does not affect cats who live with other cats as often as single cats, but it is possible, especially in individuals who were orphaned or weaned too young. The behaviors associated with separation anxiety usually begin 8 to 12 hours after the owner leaves home. They include:

- inappropriate elimination, often near the door through which you leave or on something the cat associates with you

- stress-induced diarrhea

- anorexia

- vomiting

- loud vocalization

- excessive grooming, causing bald spots or even sores

- destructive scratching and chewing

- aggression

Relieving a cat of separation anxiety requires time, patience, and effort. The idea you want to get through to your cat is that your absence is no big deal, and you will come back. Don't fuss over him before you leave or as soon as you get back. Go about your business, leave quietly, and return quietly. Wait at least 15 minutes after you get home before feeding or cuddling the cat so that you don't reward him specifically for your return.

Having the company of at least one other cat with whom he gets along will also help. The stress of a hostile

Cat trees will provide your cats with room to lounge, explore, hide, and scratch.

relationship, though, can make things worse, so don't leave your anxious cat with a cat who picks on him. Put them in different parts of the house while you're gone.

If your cat's anxious behavior is making him ill or prone to hurting himself, or if he's become excessively destructive or aggressive, speak to your veterinarian. A short course of anti-anxiety medication may help.

Aggression

Like many families, your family of cats may not always live in perfect harmony. Inter-cat aggression takes many forms and arises from different causes, and it can make life miserable for you as well as the cats. If fights arise among your cats, you need to act quickly to prevent serious injuries and to keep hostilities from becoming permanent.

The first rule for stopping a cat fight: *Do not try to grab or handle your cats if they are agitated.* They are quick, angry or frightened, and very well armed. Your cats may swipe and bite at you without even knowing it is you, and you can be seriously injured. This goes double for children. To break up a fight, spray the cats with water or throw a thick blanket or towel over one of them before you pick him up and move him to another part of the house.

If everything was fine until you introduced one more cat, crowding may be the problem. In some cases, the addition of more vertical perches may diffuse the tension enough to stop aggression. Be sure, too, that there are enough valuable resources to go around—food and water, litter boxes, toys, scratching posts, and your attention.

If two of your cats suddenly show aggression toward one another after living peacefully together, they may be displaying fear-induced aggression. In

A cat with separation anxiety may damage your home, or worse, harm himself or your other cats.

You must separate bullies from victims before any harm comes to either party.

other words, they have become afraid of one another, usually by blaming one another for a frightening event (which is why this behavior is also known as redirected aggression). For instance, if the cats were sleeping near one another and were startled awake by a loud noise, they may each hold the other responsible. They will jump up and assume defensive postures with backs arched and hair puffed out. Each cat may think that the other is about to attack, and a fight will erupt. From then on, they may react aggressively whenever they see each other around the house.

Fear-induced aggression is best treated by separating the cats and then reintroducing them. (See Chapter 4.) Your goal is to let them get used to one another again without being afraid. Keep them in separate parts of the house without access to one another for several days. Then switch their locations so that they become reacquainted with one another's scents, and proceed with the reintroduction process.

Another type of inter-cat aggression is often called territorial, but it may have more to do with the aggressor's journey through adolescence into adulthood than it does with territory. The aggressor in these cases is usually from nine months to two years old. The victim is often a newcomer but may be a cat with whom the aggressor has lived peacefully in the past. The aggression usually starts with hissing, growling, and posturing, followed by

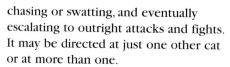

chasing or swatting, and eventually escalating to outright attacks and fights. It may be directed at just one other cat or at more than one.

If one of your cats begins to bully another, you need to protect the victim so that he doesn't develop stress-related behaviors. Fear often causes victimized cats to hide and to avoid places where they might be attacked, including the litter box and food and water bowls. Make sure that the cat or cats being picked on have safe quarters. Then, take steps to stop the aggression.

Don't yell at the aggressor; you'll frighten all your cats, not just him. Keep several large squirt bottles filled with water in strategic locations, and the moment he begins to behave aggressively, soak him with the water. (Don't spray the victim!) If you are consistent and your timing and aim are good, he'll decide that being a bully

isn't all that much fun. If that doesn't do the trick, speak to your vet or ask for a referral to a feline behaviorist, who can observe your cats and recommend an effective solution.

Although we don't hear about cat bites as often as we do dog bites, cats sometimes behave aggressively toward people. If one of your cats becomes aggressive, the first thing you need to do is to keep yourself and your family safe. Confine your cat in a closed room, or if necessary, a carrier, and then take him to the vet for a checkup. Illness or pain can cause even the sweetest cat to react defensively when handled.

Fear can also trigger defensive aggression. A cornered cat may hiss, spit, swat, and bite to protect himself. Teach children never to corner a cat or do anything else to frighten one. Teach them also that some cats just don't want to be petted and to leave cats alone when they walk away or are sleeping, eating, or caring for kittens. Supervise all interaction between young children and your cats, and teach older children to recognize cat talk for "leave me alone"—growling, tail or skin twitching, stiff posture, ears pulled back, claws unsheathed. Animals, especially dogs, can also cause aggressive behavior in cats who are not interested in being sniffed or otherwise bothered, so train your dog not to chase the cats, and be sure that the cats have dog-free zones.

Stress can cause aggressive reactions in some cats, so see if something in the environment may be causing your cat or cats to react. Whatever you do, never punish your cat physically. Doing so will make the problem worse.

When and Where to Seek Help

If your cats, individually or collectively, develop a behavioral problem that you can't correct quickly, seek professional help before bad habits become thoroughly ingrained or the behavior becomes overwhelming for you and the rest of your family.

Start by speaking to your veterinarian to rule out a physical cause. If your cat is healthy, ask for a referral to a qualified feline behaviorist. Ask for references and check them— anyone can claim to be a behaviorist. You need to find someone who has training and successful experience working with cats who have had problems similar to the one your cat or cats are exhibiting.

Chapter 7

Keeping All Your Cats

Healthy

All cats should get regular veterinary care, and it is especially important in a multi-cat environment. Without good preventive care and quick response to signs of trouble, infectious diseases and parasites can spread quickly through a household. If you work with your veterinarian and give your cats good health care, along with lots of love, they should live long, healthy lives and be better companions for you and for one another.

Help Your Vet Help Your Cats

You are your cats' first line of defense. If you notice a change in health or behavior, write down the following information and give it to your vet. Detailed information can make diagnosis easier and may save one or more lives.

Note for each affected cat when you first saw each physical or behavioral change; whether symptoms occur all the time or sporadically; if the symptom is sporadic, how often it occurs; how long the symptom lasts each time it occurs; what was happening around each cat when the symptom occurred; and any unusual events in the previous few weeks (new carpet, lawn treatment, change in household cleaning products, new flea product, arrival or departure of a member of the household, and so on).

The Right Veterinarian

You need the right veterinarian to help you keep your cats healthy and to treat them when they are not. It's hard to believe, but cats are not every vet's favorite clients, so take the time to find

one who genuinely likes cats. Beyond that, she should listen to your concerns and answer your questions clearly and in as much detail as you want. Let's look at some criteria you can use to evaluate your current or prospective veterinarian and vet practice.

The Right Atmosphere

Most vets work in multi-vet practices, and the climate of the practice is as important as the individual veterinarian you use. If your cats are uncomfortable around dogs, consider using a cats-only practice. Other factors to consider when choosing a practice might include some or all of the following:

- What are the facility's hours?

- What arrangements are there for emergency care outside regular hours?

- Can you choose which vet you will see? Can you see someone else if your regular vet is not available?

- Can you get an appointment on short notice in a serious but nonemergency situation?

- Are you comfortable with the facility's payment and billing practices?

- Does it offer a discount for multiple cats or multiple pets?

- Does it push annual vaccinations or promote more current vaccination protocols?

- Can you drop your cats off and pick them up later if necessary? Can you see the vet?

- Does the facility offer other services

that you may want to use, such as boarding or grooming?

You may have additional concerns, and the vet and the office manager should be willing to answer whatever questions you have. After all, you will be paying for their services and entrusting the lives of your feline family to them.

Alternative Veterinary Practices

More and more cat owners and veterinarians are turning to alternative, complementary, or holistic veterinary practices, including the formal disciplines of chiropractic, acupuncture, homeopathy, herbal therapy, and nutrition, and the less formal practices of massage therapy, TTouch, shiatsu, reiki, and others. The common thread that runs through these approaches is the belief that emotional and physical factors affect health. Some alternative practices and practitioners are safe and beneficial, but some are not, so be cautious in choosing for your cats.

If you need to find a new vet, begin by asking your cat-owning relatives, friends, and neighbors who they use. Local shelters, rescue programs, cat breeders, and cat clubs may also refer you to their favorites. You might also ask if there is any vet or practice they avoid, and why. Finally, check the yellow pages or Internet, particularly if you are looking for a cats-only or alternative practice.

Routine Preventive Care

One of the most important things you can do for your cats' health is to take each one to the vet at least once a year for a thorough physical examination. Early detection can keep many health problems from getting out of control, saving you money and heartache.

A routine "well-cat" exam usually takes less than half an hour. During a routine veterinary examination, your veterinarian will check your cat's:

- teeth and gums for tartar, swelling, or inflammation
- ears for infection, ear mites, or other problems

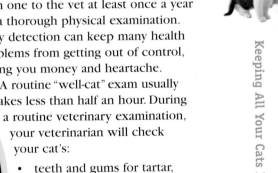

Most vets will cut your cats' nails if you are uncomfortable doing the job.

- eyes for pupil response and retinal appearance
- skin and coat for parasites and other problems
- weight, temperature, respiration, and heart rate
- blood chemistry
- fecal sample for intestinal parasites

She will also give vaccinations and prescribe heartworm prevention and other medications as needed.

You might want to schedule more than one cat for the same visit to save time (and possibly money—be sure to ask), or you may want to spread the expense of multiple exams over the course of the year. Whatever you choose, keep track of each cat's records and schedule—not always easy if you have several cats. I keep a separate file folder for each of my pets, and I use my computer calendar to remind me to schedule appointments.

Infectious Diseases and Vaccination

As many cat owners know, there have been much concern and discussion in recent years about health and behavior problems associated with excessive vaccination. In response to the evidence, the American Veterinary Medical Association (AVMA), the American Association of Feline Practitioners (AAFP), most veterinary colleges, and many veterinarians and owners have changed their vaccination schedules for cats and other pets. Although vaccine

FAMILY-FRIENDLY TIP

Kids and Vet Visits

Visits to the vet can be scary not only for your cat but for your child as well. However, they are also a good opportunity to teach kids several lessons. You can prepare your children by explaining the following points before vet visits:
- Preventive health care is important for cats and for people.
- Examinations are an important part of preventive health care.
- Pet ownership involves responsibility as well as play.
- Shots hurt but keep us from getting sick.

Good manners are important when meeting animals as well as people. Never approach without permission, and then do so slowly, quietly, and gently.

manufacturers usually recommend annual revaccination, the AAFP now recommends that most cats receive core vaccines every three years. The exception is rabies vaccination, which by law is required every year or every three years in most states and many countries, although a study is now underway to evaluate the long-term effectiveness of rabies vaccines with an eye to less frequent vaccination.

Vaccines are divided into two categories: core and noncore. All cats should receive the core vaccinations, which protect against diseases to which cats are commonly exposed. Whether one or more of your cats should receive noncore vaccines for protection against less common diseases depends on each cat's age, health status, breed, potential for exposure to the disease, and the type of vaccine. Keep in mind that even if only one of your cats ever ventures outdoors, he can carry home diseases and parasites that can attack your whole feline family.

Before you decide that it's too risky to vaccinate your cats, it's important to remember that vaccines, used properly, are still the best line of defense against infectious disease. Because you have more than one cat, if one acquires a contagious disease, the others probably will, too. The best thing you can do for your cats is to educate yourself about the benefits and risks of vaccination, work with your vet to decide which vaccines to give, and establish a schedule for each cat.

Parasite Control

Parasites are everywhere, and they spread easily from one host animal to another. You can bet that if you find signs of fleas, worms, or other nasty little creatures on one of your cats, your other cats are infected, too. Talk to your vet about prevention, and if you spot a parasite that has slipped past your defenses, contact your vet. You may need to treat all your cats (and other pets), as well as your home and yard. With vigilance and quick action, you can win the battles, if not the war,

Thorough research and recommendations will lead you to the right vet for you and your cats.

Symptoms That Require Veterinary Attention

If any of your cats has the following symptoms, contact your veterinarian.

- fever
- depression
- loss of appetite or difficulty eating, drinking, or swallowing
- unexplained weight loss or gain
- vomiting
- diarrhea
- difficulty urinating, accidents, or a change in the color, odor, or amount of urine
- dehydration
- continual sneezing
- watery eyes
- discharge from nose and eyes
- difficulty breathing or breathing through the mouth
- coughing
- blisters or ulcers on the tongue
- listlessness
- weakness
- reduced stamina
- paralysis
- abnormal aggression
- lumps or swellings that persist or grow larger
- difficulty breathing
- lameness or stiffness that lasts more than a day or two
- difficulty defecating
- sores that do not heal
- bleeding or discharge
- offensive or unusual odor

and keep your cats safe from parasites. Let's look at some of the most common parasites of cats and what you can do to fend them off.

Fleas

These nasty little bloodsucking insects are not just annoying—they also carry deadly diseases and parasites. They can leap vast distances, making them hard to catch, and if you do snag one, its hard shell makes it hard to squish. If that's not enough, flea eggs and larvae can survive long periods without food only to "wake up" when a potential victim comes along.

Rabies in Cats

According to the Centers for Disease Control (CDC), 7,437 cases of rabies in animals were reported in the continental US and Puerto Rico in 2001. The number of cases of rabies in cats increased 8.4 percent, while cases in all other domestic animals decreased, and more than twice as many cases of rabies occurred in cats as in dogs or cattle.

Kittens are more susceptible to illness than full-grown cats. Pay close attention to your kitten's behavior, and if you notice a change and feel that something is wrong, write down the details and contact your veterinarian.

Vaccination for Cats

Core vaccinations for cats defend against the
following diseases:

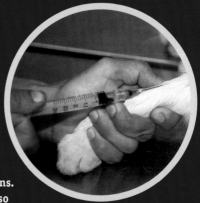

- Rabies is a viral disease that can affect any mammal,
  including people. Rabies is fairly common in wild
  animals and is transmitted through an infected
  animal's saliva, which outdoor cats can easily
  encounter. The rabies virus attacks the central
  nervous system and takes two forms. Furious rabies
  is what most of us picture: a highly aggressive animal
  foaming at the mouth. Dumb rabies causes paralysis of
  the lower jaw, then the limbs, and finally the vital organs.
  Once the symptoms appear, the disease is always fatal, so
  prevention is essential.

- Feline panleukopenia (feline distemper) is a common, often fatal viral disease. Most cats
  will be exposed to it at some time, so vaccination is critical. Kittens who are exposed to
  panleukopenia in utero or during their first months often suffer permanent brain damage
  and other lifelong problems.

- Feline viral rhinotracheitis (FVR) is a very common severe upper respiratory viral infection.
  Vaccination won't prevent the disease but will make its symptoms less severe.

- Feline calicivirus (FCV) is an extremely common viral disease of the upper respiratory
  system. An infected cat may carry the virus and display symptoms (runny eyes and
  sneezing) throughout his life, even with treatment.

When at risk of exposure, cats are commonly given noncore vaccinations for the
following diseases:

- Feline leukemia virus (FeLV) is a viral disease that suppresses the immune system, putting
  its victim at increased risk for lymphoma, other cancers, and various bacterial and viral
  diseases. It is one of the leading causes of serious illness and death in domestic cats. The
  American Association of Feline Practitioners (AAFP) recommends vaccination for cats who
  are at risk of exposure through contact with other cats.

- Feline infectious peritonitis (FIP) is a potentially fatal viral disease. It is hard to diagnose,
  but symptoms may include jaundice, mild anemia, enlarged lymph nodes, gastrointestinal
  problems, conjunctivitis, eye ulcers, neurological impairment, depression, weight loss, fever,
  and sometimes kidney, liver, ocular, neurological, or pancreatic disease.

- chlamydia (feline chlamydophila) causes conjunctivitis and is highly contagious.

- ringworm (more on this later in the chapter)

To eliminate fleas, you need to kill them at all life stages—eggs, larvae, and adults. Ask your vet for an effective and safe flea-eradication program. Most over-the-counter flea products are not very effective, and some are hazardous to cats. You also need to be sure that the chemicals in various products used on your cats and in the environment are compatible. Some insecticides are dangerous when used together.

Ticks

Ticks are arthropods (relatives of spiders) that hang out in woods, fields, and grass—or carpets, bedding, and upholstery. When an animal comes along, they latch on, sink their pincher-like mouthparts into their victim's skin, and feast on the animal's blood. Ticks detach willingly from their hosts only when they are full. Like fleas, ticks transmit diseases and reproduce like crazy.

Ticks don't seem to affect cats as much as they do dogs, but I have found ticks on my cats. If ticks are a problem where you live, and if your cats go outdoors or you have a dog who could carry ticks into the house, take the time to inspect each of your pets every few days, especially in warm weather. (And be sure to inspect yourself, too, if you walk through high grass or brush.)

If you find a tick, remove it *carefully.* If it has not yet attached, pick it off with a tissue and flush it down the toilet. If it is attached, dab it with iodine, alcohol, or a strong saline solution to make it let go. Then grasp the tick's body with a tick remover (available from some pet-supply stores), forceps, or tweezers. Pull gently *straight out* and dispose of the tick. After you pull it out, you should see a small hole in the skin. A black spot means that the tick left its head behind (consult your vet for further instructions). Clean the bite with alcohol or iodine, and apply an antiseptic. Keep an eye on it for a few days, and call your vet if you see signs of infection. Wash your hands and any tool you used with soap and hot water.

Outdoor cats are more likely to become hosts for various parasites. When they come back inside, the parasites will infect your other cats.

Mange

Mange refers to several skin conditions caused by different species of tiny arthropods called mites. They eat skin debris, hair follicles, and tissue and can cause severe itching, hair loss, and skin flaking and sores. Animals with mange often scratch themselves raw, opening the way for viral, fungal, or parasitic infections. Cats are susceptible to three types of mange.

- Notoedric mange (sarcoptic mange or scabies) is caused by a microscopic mite that burrows under the skin to lay eggs. Within three weeks the eggs hatch, and the larvae develop rapidly into adults that soon lay their own eggs. Scabies can cause extensive hair loss, is highly contagious, and affects cats, other animals, and people.

- Cheyletiellosis ("walking dandruff") is caused by white mites that look like dandruff. It is unattractive and highly contagious but easy to treat.

- Demodectic mange (demodex) is rare in cats but can occur in felines with compromised immune systems. Demodex is not considered to be highly contagious.

Mange, especially scabies and cheyletiellosis, can quickly become a serious problem in a multi-cat household, so if you suspect that one of your cats has any form of mange, get him to the vet immediately. Don't rely on over-the-counter or home remedies. Treatment must be geared to the specific type of mite to be effective, and it's essential to learn how

Managing Meds

If you have cats taking different medications, it's important to know who is supposed to get how much of what how often. You must also keep track of whether anyone has been given a particular dose. Here are some tips for keeping it all straight:

- Keep all cat medications in a central location. Keep *all* medications in secure locations where cats and other pets cannot get at them.

- Label all medications clearly with the name of the cat. Prescription labels are often small, so make the name big enough to read easily.

- If you have several cats taking several meds each day, create a weekly or monthly chart and post it near the medications. List each cat, his meds, and the times he should take each. Then check off each dose.

- If you keep medications that you use irregularly, check the expiration dates from time to time and carefully dispose of drugs that are out of date.

to protect the rest of your household from infection.

Ringworm

Ringworm is not a worm at all but a highly contagious fungus that spreads easily from one victim to another. It infects cats, other pets, and people. Animals with ringworm tend to scratch themselves raw, and secondary infections are common.

Ringworm often appears first as a sore-looking bald circle. Fungal infections like ringworm are hard to treat and harder to cure, so don't waste time and money on over-the-counter or home remedies. Your vet can make an accurate diagnosis, prescribe effective drugs, and advise you on ways to keep ringworm from spreading through your household.

Intestinal Parasites

Like all living creatures, cats are vulnerable to several species of parasitic intestinal worms, some of which can threaten your cats' health. If one of your cats has worms, they probably all do, and they should all be treated at the same time to eliminate the parasites.

As always, it's important to use safe and effective medication designed to eliminate the specific parasite, so if you find evidence of worms in the litter boxes or elsewhere, put a specimen in a plastic bag and take it to the vet for identification. Even if you don't see evidence of worms, take a fecal specimen from each of your cats to your vet at least annually. If your cats go outdoors, they can acquire parasites from wild animals and should have fecal exams every three months.

The two parasites you are most like to spot are roundworms and tapeworms. They are visible to the naked eye and are very common.

Your veterinarian will prescribe all necessary medications if your cats fall ill or are infected by parasites.

Not all Heartworm Medications Are the Same

If you have a dog as well as cats, they all need to take heartworm preventive medicines if the parasite is present where you live. But their medications are not interchangeable. *Do not* treat your cats with your dog's heartworm medicine, or vice versa.

Roundworms look like 8-inch (20-cm) strands of spaghetti. They are carried by many kinds of animals and can be spread easily from one cat to another in a multi-cat home. Kittens often acquire roundworms from their mothers. Although they don't attack the host directly, roundworms eat food passing through the host animal's digestive system and can cause nausea, vomiting, and diarrhea. A large infestation can cause anemia and malnutrition.

Tapeworms can grow several feet (meters) long but are more difficult to diagnose than most worms because they do not typically show up in feces. Infected animals do, however, pass small, white worm segments in bowel movements, and these rice-like segments often stick to fur around the host's anus. Occasionally longer sections are passed with stools. Tapeworms begin life in intermediate hosts—fleas, mice, rabbits, and other

animals. When your cat eats an infected animal, it ingests tapeworm larvae, which mature inside your cat. A special medication is needed to eliminate tapeworms.

Several other types of internal parasites also affect cats, especially those who go outdoors. Some are too small to see without a microscope, but they can cause weight loss, anemia, respiratory infection, and diarrhea. If one of your cats has these symptoms, see your vet and take a fecal specimen along.

Heartworm

Heartworms are long, thin parasitic worms that can infest the hearts of cats, dogs, and even people. Mosquitoes ingest the microscopic heartworm larvae when they suck the blood of infected animals, and they then pass the larvae to new victims. The larvae move through the animal's blood vessels to the heart, where they reproduce. As they increase in number and size, the worms damage the cardiovascular system, cause congestive heart failure, and eventually kill the host. Symptoms of heartworm disease range from none at all in the early stages to vague unwellness to coughing and other signs of congestive heart failure.

Heartworm has been identified in all parts of the US, and because mosquitoes can find their way indoors, heartworm disease affects indoor as well as outdoor cats. All of your cats should be checked every year or two for heartworm infection. Ask your vet

Cats spend a lot of time grooming themselves.

whether they should take heartworm medicine as well.

Grooming for Good Health

Most cats are very clean, and they work hard to keep themselves that way. Even so, regular grooming is important, and in a multi-cat home it becomes an even more crucial part of a comprehensive approach to cat care and housekeeping. Grooming sessions also give each of your cats some private time with you, strengthening the bond between you and each of them.

Coat and Skin Care

Regardless of individual differences among your cats, healthy skins and coats start with good nutrition, health care, and parasite control. Assuming that those basic requirements are in place, regular brushing enhances their benefits by stimulating the sebaceous (oil) glands and distributing the oils to lubricate your cats' skins and coats. Careful brushing and combing also eliminate tangles in long coats before they turn into mats that can harbor parasites and trap heat and moisture, leading to sores and infections. And unless you have hairless cats, you know that cats shed. Brushing helps control the furry fallout that would otherwise blanket your floors, furniture, and clothing. Finally, brushing helps prevent hairballs, the bane of cat owners, especially those with several cats who groom not only themselves but also each other.

Most cats don't need to be bathed

How to Prevent Hairballs

When cats lick themselves and one another, they swallow hair, which they can't digest. The hairs glom together into icky balls. Most cats cough up their hairballs with no ill effects (except to the couch or carpet where it lands). In some cats, though, hairballs cause vomiting, constipation, loss of appetite, and blockages that require surgical removal. You can reduce the incidence of hairballs in your cats by brushing them frequently and by feeding food designed to prevent hairballs. If your cats seem to have a lot of hairballs, ask your vet for advice.

very often, but baths are sometimes necessary to fight a flea invasion or clean up a cat who has gotten into a toxic or otherwise yucky substance. Regular rinsing or bathing also removes allergens from your cats' fur, making it possible for some people with allergies to tolerate cats in the house. Some cats actually enjoy a bath, and most will at least learn to tolerate the process.

Brush each cat thoroughly before his bath. Use lukewarm water and a mild shampoo formulated for cats. Rinse thoroughly; soap residue can cause skin problems and may make your cats sick if they ingest it when grooming themselves. If you have long-haired cats, comb or brush their coats while still damp. Keep your cats warm and away from drafts until they are completely dry.

Nail Care

Your cats' claws grow constantly (unless they have been declawed). New growth on each claw is covered with a protective layer that is removed by scratching, preferably on a scratching post rather than your doorframes or upholstery. (See Chapter 6.) Regular trimming will help keep your cats' claws and paws healthy and reduce the chances of injury during play or in a family squabble. You can purchase nail clippers made for cats if you'd like—I've always used a standard nail clipper made for people.

Begin by getting your cats used to having their paws handled. Some cats don't mind at all; others may need from several days to several weeks to be really comfortable with letting you hold and handle their paws. Be patient, gentle, and persistent, and your cats will come around. When each cat is okay, begin trimming. If a particular cat is nervous about the process, do just one or two nails at a time until he relaxes. If he is wriggly, wrap him in a towel with only his head and the paw you are trimming exposed. Put your index finger on the toe pad and your thumb on top of the paw, and gently press to extend the claw from the sheath.

Trim only the sharp tip of the claw. It has no nerves, so trimming it doesn't hurt. The quick—the living center of the claw— does contain nerves and blood, and if you cut into it, your cat will bleed and experience pain. The quick is darker, or sometimes pinker, than the rest of the claw. If you accidentally cut into the quick, you can usually stop any bleeding by dipping the claw in styptic powder (available from veterinarians, pet-supply stores, or the shaving section of many other stores) or cornstarch. (If bleeding continues for longer than ten minutes, or if the blood is spurting, call your vet.) Trim the front claws, including the dewclaws (the small ones on the front legs above the feet). Rear claws don't need to be trimmed as often, if ever. They aren't as sharp as the front ones, and they grow more slowly.

Ear Care

When cats live together, and especially if they play and sleep together, it's easy for them to pass some types of ear infections from one to another. To keep their ears healthy, check each of your cat's ears at least once a week, and clean them as necessary to prevent ear mites; allergies; and bacterial, fungal, and yeast infections.

Check the inner part of your cat's pinna—the fleshy triangle that we call the ear—by holding the tip with your thumb and forefinger and rolling it

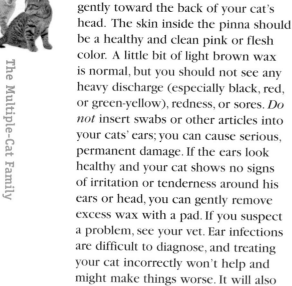

The Multiple-Cat Family

gently toward the back of your cat's head. The skin inside the pinna should be a healthy and clean pink or flesh color. A little bit of light brown wax is normal, but you should not see any heavy discharge (especially black, red, or green-yellow), redness, or sores. *Do not* insert swabs or other articles into your cats' ears; you can cause serious, permanent damage. If the ears look healthy and your cat shows no signs of irritation or tenderness around his ears or head, you can gently remove excess wax with a pad. If you suspect a problem, see your vet. Ear infections are difficult to diagnose, and treating your cat incorrectly won't help and might make things worse. It will also allow some infections more time to spread to your other cats.

Dental Care

Good dental care is important throughout your cats' lives. Cats are such masters at hiding their discomfort that they may go for months with undetected dental problems—which means that regular examinations are critical. Broken or loose teeth, gum disease, abscesses, and decay are not only painful but may contribute to health and behavior problems.

Periodontal (gum) disease is very common in cats. Every time your cats eat, bacteria and food particles accumulate along their gum lines and under their gums, forming plaque. If it remains, the plaque hardens into calculus, which irritates the gums and leads to infection and loss of teeth and bone. Bacteria from unhealthy gums can also travel through the blood to the heart, kidneys, and other organs, leading to serious disease.

Regular preventive dental care will keep your cats' teeth and gums healthy and enhance the length and quality of their lives. It's never too late to begin. An oral examination should be part of each cat's regular physical exam. Your vet may suggest periodic professional cleanings under anesthesia. This does pose some risk, but new anesthetics are much safer than the older ones. Ask your vet what kind of anesthetic she uses, how easy it is to reverse, and how your cat will be monitored during the procedure.

In addition to professional cleaning, you can learn to brush your cats' teeth—honest! Ask your vet to show you how. Daily brushing is ideal, but even two or three brushings a week will keep teeth and gums healthier and give you an opportunity to spot foul breath, loose or missing teeth, sores, lumps, and other problems that may need veterinary attention. You can purchase specially designed toothbrushes, "finger" brushes, or cleaning pads for your cats. Each cat should have his own brush to avoid spreading bacteria. Use toothpaste designed for cats—human toothpaste and baking soda can make them sick.

Chapter 8

Managing the

Unthinkable

Life isn't all catnip and salmon, for people or for cats, but you can do a lot to help your cats live longer, safer, and more comfortable lives. This chapter discusses how you can protect your cats from hazards and what to do in a crisis.

Basic First Aid for Cats

When you live with more than one cat, the odds are that you will need some basic first-aid supplies once in a while. Pet supply stores offer ready-made pet first-aid kits, but you can easily assemble one yourself. Here are the essential ingredients of a kitty first-aid kit:

- muzzle designed for cats or a towel or small blanket to wrap a frightened cat or cover a wound— one for each of your cats
- 3% hydrogen peroxide—write the purchase date on the label, and discard and replace the bottle once a year
- medicine syringe for administering liquids
- directions and telephone numbers for your regular veterinarian and the closest emergency veterinary clinic

- telephone number for the National Animal Poison Control Center (NAPCC): 1-888-4-ANI-HELP or 1-900-680-0000
- small rectal thermometer
- lubricant, such as plain K-Y
- sterile saline eye solution to flush eyes
- broad-spectrum antibiotic cream
- small bottle of mild liquid dish detergent to remove contaminants from coat and skin
- disposable gloves to protect your hands if you need to handle a contaminated cat
- tweezers
- scissors
- basic veterinary first-aid manual (ask your veterinarian or local Red Cross for recommendations)

If you keep your supplies in a portable box, they'll be easy to find and take along if you leave home with your cats.

Cats, bold and curious as they are, sometimes get themselves into trouble despite our efforts to safeguard them. Most injuries are not life threatening, but there are

If you have to take your cats to the veterinarian because of illness or injury, put only one cat in each crate. Confinement and pain are the perfect ingredients for violent biting and scratching. However, two healthy cats in an appropriately sized crate is fine.

Hot Cats, Cool Cats

An adult cat's normal body temperature is 100° to 102.5°F (38° to 39°C). A newborn kitten's temperature should be 96° to 97°F (35.5° to 36°C).

times when knowing what to do can make the difference between life and death. If you find yourself faced with a feline emergency, protect yourself (a frightened cat won't be rational and may injure you), then focus on helping your cat. Try not to panic.

We have room here only for very basic information, so I encourage you to purchase a good book on veterinary first aid to keep with your first-aid kit. You might also want to take a course on pet first aid from your local Red Cross or other source. Now let's consider some common feline emergencies.

Bites and Scratches

Bites, scratches, and other lacerations aren't uncommon among cats, especially if they live with other cats or spend time outdoors. If a wound appears to be minor, clean it gently with a clean cloth dampened with water. *Do not* put hydrogen peroxide on an open wound; it will make bleeding harder to stop and can damage tissue. If the wound is bleeding, apply direct pressure with a clean towel, cloth, or gauze pad. When the bleeding stops or slows, apply a broad-spectrum topical antibiotic. No matter how minor the wound, *call your vet.* Bites and scratches introduce bacteria, and your cat may need additional antibiotics to prevent infection.

If the wound is deep or long or won't stop bleeding, your cat needs immediate veterinary attention. Keep pressure on the wound if it is bleeding, and get your cat to the vet. Have someone else drive if possible so that you can continue to apply pressure. If you're on your own, put your cat in a carrier to keep him secure. You can tape a gauze pad to the wound, but *do not* apply a tourniquet unless you have had first-aid training. Improper use of a tourniquet can cause serious, permanent damage.

Wounds that don't bleed are also dangerous, especially bites or scratches from other animals, because teeth and claws introduce bacteria that remain in the tissue. If your cat has been in a fight, talk to your vet. She will probably prescribe an oral antibiotic. If he is bitten by a wild or stray animal, he may be at risk for rabies (see Chapter 7), which puts your entire human and animal family at risk. Talk to your vet.

Even if your injured cat is taking antibiotics, check him carefully every day for a week or so, and let your vet know about any swelling, tenderness, or other signs of infection.

Should You Call Your Veterinarian?

situations are life threatening and require immediate action; others allow you a bit
time. Here's how to decide:

your cat to the vet immediately if he has any of the following symptoms:

- lack of heartbeat
- severe difficulty breathing
- bluish or very pale tongue or gums
- a broken bone
- heavy bleeding
- a severe wound
- an injured eye
- a wound, or multiple wounds, from a fight, especially with another
  cat or an unidentified or unvaccinated animal
- a puncture wound, especially to the chest or abdomen
- a bullet or arrow wound
- head trauma
- trauma from a vehicle or other fast-moving object or from a fall from a high place
- bite from a snake, scorpion, or spider
- biting, licking, or mouthing a poisonous toad or other amphibian
- porcupine quills
- broken tooth (if a healthy tooth is knocked out and you have it, keep it in milk and
  get to the vet)
- hives or swelling, especially on the face
- electrical shock
- burn or smoke inhalation from a fire
- temperature above 105°F (40.5°C)
- frostbite
- choking
- swallowing an inedible object, including yarn or string
- repeated vomiting or vomiting blood
- severe diarrhea or diarrhea with a foul smell
- blood in feces or dark, tarry-looking feces
- blood in urine
- repeated and unsuccessful straining to urinate or defecate

- bleeding from the urinary, genital, or rectal region or tissue protruding from the rectum
- crying when trying to urinate or a male licking continuously at his genitals
- suspected poisoning or overdose of medication
- collapse, extreme lethargy, or loss of consciousness
- seizures
- staggering, walking in circles, inability to bear weight on a leg, or other abnormal movement
- rapid side-to-side eye movement or tilted head
- severe or continuous pain

Call your vet the same day if your cat has any of the following symptoms:
- congestion or rapid or shallow breathing (except right after exercise)
- continuous coughing or sneezing
- excessive drinking or refusal to drink for more than a day
- loss of appetite for more than a day
- diarrhea or repeated vomiting for more than a day
- sudden behavioral change, including unusual aggression or crying
- severe lameness
- red or cloudy eyes, squinting, or apparent vision problems
- swollen testicles or scrotum
- excessive shedding, head shaking, or scratching
- red, tender, or hot-feeling lumps
- clear signs of parasites, or maggots
- nosebleeds or easy bruising

Call your vet within a few days if your cat has any of the following symptoms:
- loss of appetite but no other symptoms
- rapid weight loss or gain
- soft stool (without blood, foul odor, mucus, or green or black color)
- drooling
- foul breath
- sporadic vomiting (without blood or abdominal tenderness)
- lameness lasting more than a day
- swollen joints
- depression, lethargy, change in sleep habits, unusual lack of interest in play or exercise
- itching or unpleasant body odor
- discharge from the eye, ear, or other orifice

Common Poisons

Although the following list of poisons is frighteningly long, it does not include every danger. The best cure is prevention, so keep these and other hazardous products locked up where your cats cannot get to them.

- Rodent poisons, coyote bait, slug bait, ant and roach bait, and other antipest poisons that are made to attract and kill animals. A single dose of modern anticoagulant poisons, sometimes ingested by eating a dead animal, can kill a cat.

- Insecticides (including flea killers) and dewormers. Some can be absorbed through the skin on contact.

- Lead, found in paints, linoleum, batteries, lead pipe and fittings, and other products, including some metal and ceramic products produced overseas.

- Phosphorus, found in matches, matchboxes, matchbooks, flares, and fireworks.

- Petroleum products.

- Household cleaners, drain cleaners, and solvents, particularly those containing pine oil, phenol, acids, or lye.

- Some species of spiders, scorpions, snakes, and amphibians are venomous. If you know that your cat has been bitten or stung, or has picked up a poisonous toad or other creature, or if you notice a sudden swelling on his face or body, especially with evidence of penetration, get him to the vet immediately. If you kill the biter, bring the body with you.

- Medications meant for people and other pets, and overdoses of their own medications, can kill cats. Many cats are treated for poisoning from pain relievers (one acetaminophen tablet can kill an adult cat), antihistamines, sleeping pills, diet pills, heart preparations, vitamins, and other medications. Don't give your cat any medication without your vet's approval, and store all medications in a safe place.

- Tobacco products.

- More than 700 house, garden, and wild plants are toxic, including many common species. Ask your veterinarian or agricultural agent for a list for your area.

- Some foods, especially chocolate and products with caffeine (coffee, tea, many soft drinks, and other products), are toxic for cats.

- Antifreeze (ethylene glycol) tastes sweet, and a teaspoonful can kill a cat. Animals sometimes appear to recover only to die later from kidney failure.

Fractures

All fractures—broken bones—should be treated as soon as possible by a veterinarian to prevent further damage and relieve pain. If one of your cats suffers a fall, traumatic blow, or other violent event, broken bones and internal injuries are possible. Don't rely on the old notion that broken bones can't be walked on; I can tell you from experience that they can.

If you know or suspect that your cat has broken a bone, wrap him gently but securely in a blanket or towel to keep him quiet and calm, and get him to a vet. The specific treatment will depend on the type of fracture, its location and severity, and your cat's age.

Poisoning

In the best of all worlds, your cats will never have access to toxins, but the fact is that an amazing number of potentially lethal substances can be found in and around most of our homes. Unfortunately, if one cat gets into something, chances are at least one of the others will, too. Knowing the symptoms of poisoning and what to do if you think one of your cats has been poisoned can save his life.

Contact a veterinarian immediately if you know or suspect that one of your cats has been poisoned. *Do not wait* for symptoms to appear; by then, it may be too late. If possible, give your vet the container or a sample of the substance, or write down the active ingredients, brand name, manufacturer's name and telephone number, and any antidote information provided on the package. If there's any chance that one or more of your other cats have also been exposed, take all of them to the vet.

Symptoms of poisoning depend on the poison, the amount the cat has been exposed to, the size of the cat, and other factors and may include one or more of the following: vomiting, diarrhea, loss of appetite, swelling of the tongue and other mouth tissues, excessive salivation, staggering, or seizures.

Even if you don't keep a particular poison in your home or yard, your neighbors may, and if your cats go outdoors, they will be exposed to many dangers. The bottom line is that you—and your cats—are better safe than sorry, so if you suspect that one or more of your feline friends have been exposed to a poison, seek veterinary help immediately.

Disaster Preparedness

Emergencies happen whether you're home or not. Having more than one cat in your home can make their rescue more difficult, but you can increase the chances that your cats and other pets will survive an emergency whether you are there or not.

Rescue workers can't help your pets if they don't know about them, so post a notice of how many cats and other pets you have on or near the front and back doors. If your cats are likely to be outdoors, include that information, as well as their favorite indoor hidey-holes.

Make arrangements with your vet so that your cats (and other pets) can be dropped at the clinic by someone else if necessary. Sign a boarding and medical care authorization form, file one copy with your vet and one with your evacuation kit, and give copies to one or two trusted friends or neighbors. If the area where you live is prone to natural disasters, make backup arrangements for veterinary care and boarding at a safe distance as well in case the disaster affects your regular vet. If a friend or relative is willing to take responsibility for your pets, include that information.

A secure cat carrier for each of your cats could save their lives. Frightened cats can be hard to manage, and carriers provide a safe way to control and transport them. Cardboard carriers are cheap, but a panicked cat can claw and bite his way out of one, so a plastic carrier is a better investment and will

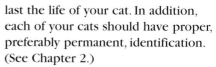

last the life of your cat. In addition, each of your cats should have proper, preferably permanent, identification. (See Chapter 2.)

Consider assembling a pet evacuation kit in a portable waterproof container. Label it clearly and keep it, along with your pet carriers, in an easily accessed place, preferably near an outside door. Your evacuation kit should hold the following items:

- A list of important phone numbers and contact information. Keep additional copies near your phone, with one or two neighbors or friends, in your car(s), and where you work.

- Each cat's veterinary records, especially copies of their rabies certificates.

- Information about any medical conditions your cats have, along with medications. Rotate medications once a month with fresh ones. If any of your cats' medications need refrigeration, include a prescription from your vet in case you cannot retrieve the medicine or store it properly during evacuation.

- Proof of ownership: your cats' license tag numbers, microchip and/or tattoo numbers, vet records, and if pertinent, registration certificate or proof of purchase or adoption.

- A data sheet for each cat including name, color and coat type, sex, age, feeding instructions, health-care needs, and a recent color photo.

- A three-day supply of cat food in cans, sealed bags, or airtight containers, as well as one or two bottles of water. Rotate food and water once a month with fresh supplies.

- Enough cash or travelers' checks to pay for boarding your cats for at least three days. You may need to pay a deposit, and cash can be hard to access during a crisis.

Hopefully, you'll never need your evacuation kit, but knowing it's there if you ever do can be reassuring.

Losing a Family Member

The relatively short time we spend with our cats is the price we pay for the joy and love they bring us while they are here. Saying farewell is never

It is hard to consider, but the time will come when you may have to say goodbye to each of your cats. Surround yourself with family and your close friends to make the best decision for them.

easy, but we can take comfort in knowing that, when the time comes, we can give our cats the final loving gift of dignity and freedom from pain.

Deciding That the Time Has Come

If one of your cats is debilitated by illness, serious injury, or old age, you may have to consider euthanasia. As long as your cat is not in severe pain, you will probably have a little time reach a decision. I have bid many cats farewell over the years, and I can tell you that there is a good chance that your cat will tell you what to do.

Quality of life should be the first and most important factor you consider. If your cat seems to be depressed, withdrawn, or in pain, or if he no longer seems interested in his housemates or simple pleasures like eating or cuddling, then it's probably time to talk to your veterinarian.

Give your vet detailed information about your cat's physical and behavioral symptoms. Old age itself can't be overcome, but many of the medical problems it brings can be treated, at least for a while. Before you opt for an expensive or invasive procedure, though, consider carefully not only how long your cat's life may be prolonged but also how well he will enjoy it. A longer life is not always a better life, so be honest with yourself and with your vet about your ability to take on the financial, physical, and emotional costs of special or long-term care for your cat. The right course of action for someone else may not be right for you.

Ask your vet for as much information as you need to be comfortable. The euthanasia process

Channeling Grief Into Good

For those of us who love our cats, the loss of one brings pain and grief. Although the healing process is highly personal, many people honor the departed friend by helping others in his memory. Here are some ideas for potential donations:

- a local animal shelter

- a cat rescue organization

- a feline health research project or organization (especially if your cat died of a disease for which a cure is being sought)

- an organization that helps with disaster relief for animals

- an organization that supports the human–animal bond

- an organization that helps people through the grief of losing a pet

FAMILY-FRIENDLY TIP

Helping Children
Through the Loss of a Pet

The loss of a pet is the first experience many children have with death. Psychologists confirm that it is important to acknowledge a child's feelings of loss and sadness and to allow the child to express the feelings evoked by the loss. Here are some ways to help your child (and yourself) honor those emotions and your cat at the same time.

- Hold a memorial service. If it's legal where you live, you may want to bury your cat in a special part of your yard. Or you might scatter his ashes or simply bury his collar or favorite toy. Give each person a chance to say something in his memory. You might place a plaque or statue over the spot or place a special plant there.

- Help or encourage your child to create a scrapbook or photo album as a memorial to your cat or to draw or color pictures of him as she remembers him. Or help her make a "memory collage" in a shadowbox frame, and let everyone in the family contribute something—a photo or two, a lock of fur, your cat's collar, name tag, or favorite toy.

- If your child is old enough, encourage her to write about your cat—a story, a poem, a letter.

- Let your child help choose the recipient of a memorial donation, and let her contribute part of the donation or make one on her own with her own money.

itself is fast and virtually painless. Give each family member a chance to say goodbye. Very young children should probably not be present for the euthanasia itself, but they should have a chance to ask questions and express their grief. If you or other family members want some time alone with your cat after the procedure, tell your vet. In addition, you will need to tell your vet how you want your cat's remains to be handled.

Your decision to be present or not is purely personal, but if you can, your cat will be more relaxed if he feels your hands and hears your voice at the end. People will give you all sorts of well-intentioned advice, but you are the only one who knows what is best for you and your cat.

Dealing With Loss

The loss of a beloved cat is a painful emotional experience. Unfortunately, some people simply do not understand the depth of feeling that can form between a person and a cat, and some will say things you don't want or need to hear. Avoid such people. Be kind to yourself, and spend time with your cats and other pets. Surround yourself with people who do understand. Channel your grief into positive activities.

If you (or anyone in your family) need someone to guide you through the grieving process, consider joining a pet-loss support group in your community or on the Internet. There you will find understanding and helpful suggestions.

Sorrow and Your Family of Cats

Not surprisingly, your other cats will very likely react emotionally to the death of one of their own. If one or more of your remaining cats had a special friendship with the one who has gone, they may experience deep grief, signaled by depression or behavioral changes. (This can happen, too, when a nonfeline family member dies or leaves.)

If you have more than one surviving cat, the dynamics of the group may shift.

Your cats may become depressed if one of their feline housemates dies. Spend extra time with them and give some extra love.

New friendships between cats may form or become closer, and territorial patterns may shift. (See Chapter 3.) In some cases, conflicts may arise. Even when there is no open conflict, you may see shifts in the individuals' social status within the group. Such changes are usually resolved in a few days as everyone adjusts.

Occasionally, a grieving cat becomes deeply depressed, especially if he spent much of his life with the deceased animal. Signs of depression include lethargy, withdrawal from normal activities, and loss of appetite. If one of your cats shows signs of depression for more than a few days, tell your vet. A short course of antidepressant medication may help. And remember, love works both ways: You are

comforted by the presence of your remaining cats, and they are comforted by you. Play and cuddle times will heal you all.

The Continuing Pleasure of Their Company

When you feel ready to add another member to your family of cats, someone will be waiting for you. He won't replace anyone else, but he'll bring his own profoundly individual felineness to fill a space in your heart and home and to enhance the social lives of your other cats.

In honor of all the cats of my life, I wish you many years of feline companionship, the rumble of purrs in your ears, and warm clowders of love.

Resources

Registry Organizations

American Association of Cat Enthusiasts (AACE)

P.O. Box 213
Pine Brook, NJ 07058
Phone: (973) 335-6717
Website: www.aaceinc.org

American Cat Fanciers Association (ACFA)

P.O. Box 1949
Nixa, MO 65714
Phone: (417) 725-1530
Website: www.acfacat.com

Canadian Cat Association (CCA)

289 Rutherford Road South
Unit 18
Brampton, Ontario, Canada L6W 3R9
Phone: (905) 459-1481
Website: www.cca-afc.com

The Cat Fanciers' Association (CFA)

1805 Atlantic Avenue
P.O. Box 1005
Manasquan, NJ 08736-0805
Phone: (732) 528-9797
Website: www.cfainc.org

Cat Fanciers' Federation (CFF)

P.O. Box 661
Gratis, OH 45330
Phone: (937) 787-9009
Website: www.cffinc.org

Fédération Internationale Féline (FIFe)

Penelope Bydlinski, General Secretary
Little Dene, Lenham Heath
Maidstone, Kent, ME17 2BS England
Phone: +44 1622 850913
Website: www.fifeweb.org

The Governing Council of the Cat Fancy (GCCF)

4-6, Penel Orlieu
Bridgwater, Somerset, TA6 3PG UK
Phone: +44 (0)1278 427 575
Website: http://ourworld.compuserve.com/homepages/GCCF_CATS/

The International Cat Association (TICA)

P.O. Box 2684
Harlingen, TX 78551
Phone: (956) 428-8046
Website: www.tica.org

Traditional and Classic Cat International (TCCI)

(formerly known as the Traditional Cat Association)

10289 Vista Point Loop
Penn Valley, CA 95946
Website: www.tccat.org

Veterinarian Specialty/ Membership Organizations

American Animal Hospital Association (AAHA)

P.O. Box 150899
Denver, CO 80215
Phone: (303) 986-2800
Website: www.aahanet.org

American Association of Feline Practitioners (AAFP)

200 4th Avenue North, Suite 900
Nashville, TN 37219
Phone: (615) 259-7788
Toll-free: (800) 204-3514
Website: www.aafponline.org

American Holistic Veterinary Medical Association (AHVMA)

2214 Old Emmorton Road
Bel Air, MD 21015
Phone: (410) 569-0795
Website: www.ahvma.org

American Veterinary Medical Association (AVMA)

1931 North Meacham Road, Suite 100
Schaumburg, IL 60173
Phone: (847) 925-8070
Fax: (847) 925-1329
Website: www.avma.org

The Academy of Veterinary Homeopathy (AVH)

P.O. Box 9280
Wilmington, DE 19809
Phone: (866) 652-1590
Website: www.theavh.org

The American Association for Veterinary Acupuncture (AAVA)

P.O. Box 419
Hygiene, CO 80533
Phone: (303) 772-6726
Website: www.aava.org

ASPCA Animal Poison Control Center

1717 South Philo Road, Suite 36
Urbana, IL 61802
Telephone: (888) 426-4435
Website: www.aspca.org

International Veterinary Acupuncture Society (IVAS)

P.O. Box 271395
Ft. Collins, CO 80527
Phone: (970) 266-0666
Website: www.ivas.org

Animal Welfare Groups and Organizations

American Humane Association (AHA)

63 Inverness Drive East
Englewood, CO 80112
Phone: (800) 227-4645
Website: www.americanhumane.org

American Society for the Prevention of Cruelty to Animals (ASPCA)

424 East 92 Street
New York, NY 10128
Phone: (212) 876-7700
Website: www.aspca.org

Best Friends Animal Sanctuary

Kanab, UT 84741-5001
Phone: (435) 644-2001
Website: www.bestfriends.org

Cats Protection

17 Kings Road
Horsham, West Sussex RH13 5PN UK
Phone: +44 (0) 1403 221900
Website: www.cats.org.uk

Feral Cat Coalition
9528 Miramar Road, PMB 160
San Diego, CA 92126
Phone: (619) 497-1599
Website: www.feralcat.com

The Winn Feline Foundation, Inc.
1805 Atlantic Avenue
P.O. Box 1005
Manasquan, NJ 08736-0805
Phone: (732) 528-9797
Website: www.winnfelinehealth.org

Websites
Acme Pet Feline Guide
www.acmepet.com/feline/index.html

ASPCA Animal Poison Control Center
1717 South Philo Road, Suite 36
Urbana, IL 61802
Telephone: (888) 426-4435
www.aspca.org

Cat Fanciers Website
www.fanciers.com

The Daily Cat
www.thedailycat.com

Healthypet
www.healthypet.com

Petfinder
www.petfinder.org
Pets 911
www.1888pets911.org

ShowCatsOnline
www.showcatsonline.com

21cats.org
http://21cats.org

VetQuest
www.vin.com/vetquest/index0.html

Publications
Animal Wellness Magazine
PMB 168
8174 South Holly Street
Centennial, CO 80122

ASPCA Animal Watch
424 East 92nd Street
New York, NY 10128

Cat Fancy Magazine
P.O. Box 52864
Boulder, CO 80322

Catnip
P.O. Box 420070
Palm Coast, FL 32142

CatWatch
P.O. Box 420235
Palm Coast, FL 32142

Whole Cat Journal
P.O. Box 1337
Radford, VA 24143

Your Cat Magazine
1716 Locust Street
Des Moines, IA 50309

Index

109

111

Index

Dedication

For my husband, Roger, born under the sign of Leo, and for George, Simon, Anniecat, Snoopy, Malcolm, Kitty, Mary, Jean-Luc, Leo, Gypsy, and Bob. Thanks for the purrs.

Acknowledgements

Many thanks to everyone with whom I've ever "talked cats" and to all the other writers, too plentiful to count, who have informed my ideas about Felis catus. Purrs and head bumps, too, for Mary Grangeia and Craig Sernotti at T.F.H., who gently scratched and patted my work into a book. You deserve a salmon dinner! Special pats for Allison Miller and the people and cats of Fort Wayne Animal Care and Control for the photo op. And, as always, my gratitude to the fascinating Family of Cats.

About the Author

Sheila Webster Boneham, Ph.D., is a life-long cat lover and owner who has written many books and articles on cat and dog care, including *Senior Cats*. Her work has appeared in national publications, including *Cat Fancy* and publications of the Cat Fanciers' Association. In 2003, the Cat Writers' Association honored Sheila's book *The Complete Idiot's Guide to Getting and Owning a Cat* with an Award of Excellence and the MUSE Award for Best Book on Care and Health. She lives in Indiana with her husband and her furry friends. You can contact her through her website www.sheilaboneham.com.

Photo Credits

Aceshot1 (Shutterstock): 36; Mohd Faizal Ahmad (Shutterstock): 4; Gregory Albertini (Shutterstock): 67; Trevor Allen (Shutterstock): 26, 70; Heather Barnhart (Shutterstock): 41; Hagit Berkovich (Shutterstock): 74; Sherri R. Camp (Shutterstock): 13; Stephanie Connell (Shutterstock): 104; Renee Davis (Shutterstock): 14; Dainis Derics (Shutterstock): 20; Arturs Dimensteins (Shutterstock): 10; Sebastian Duda (Shutterstock): 81; Isabelle Francais: 39; Carlos Gauna (Shutterstock): 105; Eric Gevaert (Shutterstock): 32; Stefan Glebowski (Shutterstock): 24, 45; Patrick Hermans (Shutterstock): 55; HTuller (Shutterstock): 100; Sara Hulan (Shutterstock): 90; Eric Isselée (Shutterstock): 40, 57 (bottom), 91, 96 (bottom), 97; Milos Jokic (Shutterstock): 29; Donald Joski (Shutterstock): 85; Julie Keen (Shutterstock): 77, 79; Andre Klopper (Shutterstock): 7; Dmitry Kosterev (Shutterstock): 30; Stuart Levine: 60; Polina Lobanova (Shutterstock): 53; Torsten Lorenz (Shutterstock): 89; Eva Madrazo (Shutterstock): 87; Patricia Malina (Shutterstock): 63; Suponev Vladimir Mihajlovich (Shutterstock): 58, 72; Debbie Oetgen (Shutterstock): 101; Alvaro Pantoja (Shutterstock): 82; Andrejs Pidjass (Shutterstock): 48; Robert Redelowski (Shutterstock): 18; Tina Rencelj (Shutterstock): 34; Robynrg (Shutterstock): 49, 57 (top), 99; Adam J. Sablich (Shutterstock): 27; Jean Schweitzer (Shutterstock): 65; Vince Serbin: 21; Dale A. Stork (Shutterstock): 43; Ferenc Szelepcsenyi (Shutterstock): 38, 52, 96 (top); Troy (Shutterstock): 103; Maxim Tupikov (Shutterstock): 83; April Turner (Shutterstock): 51, 56; John Tyson: 16; Simone van den Berg (Shutterstock): 22; Viatcheslav (Shutterstock): 92; Wolf Design: 88; Terrie L. Zeller (Shutterstock): 33; Dusan Zidar (Shutterstock): 44. All other photos courtesy of the TFH Photo Archives.

REACH OUT. ACT. RESPOND.